Teaching *for* Diversity

A Guide to Greater tanding

Third Edition

Ricardo L. García

A Joint Publication

Solution Tree

The Professional
Association in
Education

PDK

International

555 North Morton Street
Bloomington, IN 47404
800.733.6786 (toll free) / 812.336.7700
FAX: 812.336.7790

email: info@solution-tree.com
solution-tree.com

Printed in the United States of America

15 14 13 12 11   1 2 3 4 5

FSC
Mixed Sources
Product group from well-managed
forests and other controlled sources

Cert no. SW-COC-002283
www.fsc.org
© 1996 Forest Stewardship Council

Library of Congress Cataloging-in-Publication Data

García, Ricardo L.
  Teaching for diversity : a guide to greater understanding / Ricardo L. García. -- 3rd ed.
    p. cm.
  Includes bibliographical references and index.
    ISBN 978-1-935542-01-8 (perfect bound) -- ISBN 978-1-935542-02-5 (library edition)
  1. Multicultural education--United States. 2. Multicultural education--Canada. 3. Minorities--Education--United States. 4. Minorities--Education--Canada. 5. Cultural pluralism--Study and teaching. I. Title.
  LC1099.3.G367 2011
  370.1170973--dc22
                          2011014958

Solution Tree
Jeffrey C. Jones, CEO & President

Solution Tree Press
President: Douglas M. Rife
Publisher: Robert D. Clouse
Vice President of Production: Gretchen Knapp
Managing Production Editor: Caroline Wise
Copy Editor: Rachel Rosolina
Proofreader: Elisabeth Abrams
Cover and Text Designer: Amy Shock

In memory of

Walter Brunet

Beverly Caperton

Hazel Durham

Acknowledgments

This is a book of acknowledgments because so many people have contributed to it by their examples. All the book's scenarios were provided by former students, who were wrangling with issues of cultural diversity and individual differences. They are the foot soldiers in the war against ignorance. At their request, I've concealed their identities, but they will know who they are, and I hope they will see the contributions they have made. I am also indebted to Gretchen Knapp for her candid and sensitive reading of the manuscript.

Solution Tree Press would like to thank the following reviewers:

Sarah Arnold
Teacher
Elkhorn Area High School
Elkhorn, Wisconsin

Bette S. Bergeron
Dean, School of Education
Southern Illinois University
Edwardsville, Illinois

Bonnie M. Davis
Owner and Consultant
A4Achievement Consulting
Laguna Beach, California

Cynthia Gibson
Teacher
Keith High School
Orrville, Alabama

Dennis Lubeck
Executive Director
International Education
    Consortium,
    Cooperating School Districts of
    St. Louis
St. Louis, Missouri

Kay Ann Taylor
Associate Professor,
    College of Education
Kansas State University
Manhattan, Kansas

Lisa Weinbaum
Teacher
Lynn Middle School
Las Cruces, New Mexico

Table of Contents

four

Honoring Culture and Self-Identity 51

five

Reducing Prejudice 71

six

Understanding the Achievement Gap. 87

seven
Teacher as Learning-Enabler 113

eight
Linking Goals and Instructional Strategies 123

nine
Developing Curricula for Diversity 139

About the Author

 **Ricardo L. García** is a professor of education in the College of Education and Human Sciences of the University of Nebraska-Lincoln. García began his education career in 1963 as a high school English and history teacher in northern New Mexico. Since then he has continuously served in classrooms as a teacher, consultant, storyteller, and professor. In 1973, García served as codirector for the Desegregation Teacher Training Institute at Kansas State University. Since then, he has conducted research and taught in multicultural teacher education. García has tested his cross-cultural instructional theories by teaching on Native American reservations and in state penitentiaries, and by conducting bilingual family literacy programs. He also has served as a university department chair and as a central administrator of student affairs programs for diverse students and disadvantaged youth.

He is the author of numerous articles and chapters and one textbook, *Teacher in a Pluralistic Society*. In addition, he has authored four books of fiction: *Coal Camp Days*, 2001; *Brother Bill's Bait Bites Back and Other Tales From the Raton*, 2004; *Coal Camp Justice*, 2005; and *Montana's Top Bananas*, 2007.

To book Ricardo García for professional development, contact pd@solution-tree.com.

Preface to the Third Edition

eaching for Diversity: A Guide to Greater Understanding explores the big picture about teaching in contemporary society and how to foster the intellectual development of all students. It does not claim to be comprehensive in its scope; in fact, whole books have been written about the topics of each chapter. In this book, I hope to stimulate reflection about teaching in the 21st century by addressing the breadth of promises and challenges of a diverse society. *Teaching for Diversity* is not a critique of schools or society. Instead, I have chosen to cast light on what I believe teaching *can* be.

Teaching for Diversity has a new partner. Solution Tree Press is publishing the third edition in cooperation with Phi Delta Kappa International, publisher of the first two editions. In this edition, new information and updated resources have been included throughout. Chapters have been rearranged for better conceptual flow. New material in this edition includes:

- ❏ Data on and description of the impact of non-white immigration on society and schools

- ❏ Analysis and assessment of the demographic shift in American life and schools

- ❏ Analysis and description of family diversity

- ❏ Data on and analysis of religious diversity in the United States and Canada

- ❏ A new chapter devoted to teacher- and student-created curriculum materials that will reflect and support local cultures

- ❏ Reflection questions and interactive group exercises at each chapter's end

Personal teaching experiences, old and new, are woven throughout. After all, teaching is personal. That's why *Teaching for Diversity* is dedicated to three teachers who touched my life deeply: Walter Brunet, Beverly Caperton, and Hazel Durham. I hope this book will continue to strengthen understanding about the promises and challenges of teaching for diversity.

Introduction

In August 1973 I began my career as a teacher educator by working with James Boyer in the College of Education at Kansas State University, at an institute for classroom teachers whose schools were undergoing desegregation. Prior to the 1973–1974 school year, these experienced teachers had always taught in segregated schools: African American teachers taught only African American students, and white teachers taught only white students. Now they were challenged to teach students from both groups.

Everything was new. There were no mandated standards, departmental syllabi, or textbooks to guide us. We were also new to each other. Boyer and I had only recently met. The institute's teachers had been previously segregated by race and school buildings, grades 1–12. Strangers all, we knew our limitations and sensed the urgency. So we improvised, setting aside time to simply talk and ask questions. We agreed that the only bad question was the one not asked. During a discussion, a white teacher asked, "What's the best way to teach black students?"

As moderator, I looked to the other teachers.

"Funny, but I've been thinking that, too," an African American teacher said, turning the question around. "What's the best way to teach a white student?"

Out of anxiety, everyone laughed—except the two teachers. They sincerely sought an answer about how to teach students they had never taught before.

The puzzled white teacher responded, "There is no one best way to teach white students. They are all different." As the white teacher spoke, she realized she had answered her own question about black students. Students are individuals. There is no one right way to teach all of them.

Much has happened in the ensuing decades. Back in 1973, there were no personal computers or cell phones, few if any African Americans or women in high political offices, and an African American U.S. president appeared to be somewhere over the rainbow. The fundamental way of teaching is changing, too. *Mass education* has become an oxymoron. Schools are not mass production factories, nor are teachers assembly-line robots or students raw materials to be formed into widgets. Schools today assist students with integrating into society while retaining their unique personal characteristics, not assimilating by giving up their individuality. As a result, teaching is becoming a synthesis of teacher-as-information-giver and teacher-as-learning-enabler.

Many educators struggle with how to teach today's students to live in a diverse society as citizens of the larger community without doing injustice to their individual identities. That goal is a subject of this book, but not the only one. Before educators can teach their students to live in a diverse society, they must understand, engage, and embrace the diversity within their classrooms. Therefore, this book has a dual focus: how to teach diverse students, and how to teach students to deal positively with diversity.

To sharpen this focus, I have integrated two broad perspectives. The first is a perspective on the role of the teacher. Teaching for diversity calls for teachers to be enablers who foster personal responsibility in students for learning, which is an individual pursuit accomplished in cooperation with others. The teacher should not simply give information by being the sage on the stage, but at times should be the guide on the side. This is facilitative teaching based on constructivist principles: that is, the belief that humans dislike disorder and will organize ideas to make sense of them. Thus, the teacher's role is to find ways of releasing students' natural curiosities and show them how to construct meaning. As we shall see in later chapters, facilitative teaching draws from a number of antecedents, including the work of Johann Pestalozzi (1746–1827), John Dewey (1859–1952), Maria Montessori (1870–1952), and Paulo Freire (1921–1997).

The second perspective is a developmental view of human diversity. I like to think of human diversity as variations on a theme—permutations and rearrangements of the basic elements of humanity. Too often, diversity is regarded as deviations from a supposed norm. In this view, diversity is often described in pejorative terms such as *eccentric*, *deficient*, or *weird*, perhaps to be tolerated but not to be fully accepted. But these variations make each of us unique, and we would do better to learn from our differences rather than disparage or fear them. Each of us deserves all the rights and privileges of being human. Each person displays individual characteristics that, taken together, form the whole fabric of human existence. No thread in this fabric is better than another, though the threads may be different colors, different textures, and so on.

The ten chapters of *Teaching for Diversity* progress from broader notions of schools, teaching, and learning to specific practices. Each chapter ends with critical thinking exercises. The Reflections section provides questions to help readers penetrate more deeply into the chapter's key ideas. The Stand and Deliver exercises use actual cross-cultural incidents from the classrooms of experienced teachers to promote critical thinking about how to apply theories through actions.

My aim is to do more than give information and pat answers to complex issues. I hope to facilitate thoughtful discourse about teaching for diversity. In the midst of all that has changed, one thing remains true: teaching and learning are scholarly pursuits, conducted in cooperation with others. The teacher and the student are still engaged in an ongoing collaboration of the mind and heart, always creating and testing new ideas, keeping what works, discarding what does not, always blossoming, creating, and discovering.

one

What Is an American?

ays used to amble by slowly in Colfax, Nebraska. Settled in 1901 by German refugees from Russia, the small town served surrounding farms for years, but with the industrialization of agriculture and decline of subsistence farming, families moved away. Colfax tottered on the verge of extinction until the Nebraska Meat Packing Corporation (NMP) established a plant there in 2001.

Then Colfax flourished. Every nook and cranny bustled. Cracking sidewalks and empty streets were suddenly full of people coming and going on sundry errands. Abandoned stores reopened, the weathered boards of shuttered display windows were removed, and new signs were painted, such as *Carnicería, Tienda la Variedas,* and *Producios de Mexico y Centro America.*

The new merchants and customers came from Mexico and Honduras, speaking Spanish and filling the schools with their children. Overnight, a sleepy, dying German American town transformed into a vibrant community—except now Spanish rather than German is heard on the sidewalks, in stores, the library, schools, and churches.

Imagine yourself as Mrs. Davenport, a middle school teacher in this community. The majority of students speak Spanish as their first language. Your fifth-grade class consists of twelve students from Mexico, four from Honduras, and five from German American families who managed to hold on to their farms during the 1980s farm crises. English is the first and only language of the German American students. Years before, their parents were in the majority of students in school. Now these children are in the minority. Fortunately, your Spanish-speaking students have completed an English-as-a-second-language program, so you are able to teach the entire class in English.

You start each day with the Pledge of Allegiance, and then singing follows. You sit at the piano and accompany the students in "My Country, 'Tis of Thee," "America the Beautiful," or "The Star-Spangled Banner." Then you call on any student to lead a song learned at home. Somebody usually volunteers. Already everyone can sing "Happy Birthday" in both Spanish and English, and the children's version of "La Cucaracha."

All is well this morning, until Veronica Martinez enters the room on the verge of tears. How strange—her smile always lights up the room. She's one of your happiest and brightest students, but today the glimmer in her eyes is gone.

"Veronica, what's wrong?" you ask quietly.

"Oh, Mrs. Davenport," she says, "Mami and Papi have to move back to Mexico. My brothers, too."

Taken aback, you stutter, "Wait—what?"

"Yesterday, there was a raid at NMP. Papi's papers were wrong. They were forged. Mami, Papi, and Joel and Carlos . . . have to move back."

"But . . ." Your voice trails off. You're overwhelmed. The Martinez family is active in the community. Besides his job at NMP, Mr. Martinez runs a voluntary self-help group to assist newcomers into Colfax. Mrs. Martinez assists in kindergarten and first grade as a volunteer interpreter for the English-speaking teachers.

Finally, you ask, "But what about you?"

"Oh, I can stay," Veronica says. "I was born in Colfax. I'm an American. Mami and Papi want me to stay here, with Tia Julianita. She's an American, too."

"Why do they want you to stay by yourself?"

"To get a good education. You're a good teacher, you know?"

You're still in shock. How is this possible? The Martinez family is one of the best you've known since coming to Colfax. They engage in the community and give their time and abilities beyond the call of duty. Now they're breaking up!

Veronica explains that the Immigration and Naturalization Service (INS) has been conducting raids at Midwestern meatpacking plants, seeking undocumented Latinos or "illegal aliens." Veronica's parents thought they were in the United States legally, but it turns out that eight years ago, they had innocently purchased false papers from frauds pretending to be officials authorized to naturalize immigrants. The Martinez parents didn't know INS regulations and took the Spanish-speaking individuals on their word. Now they are being deported with their two older children, who were born in Mexico.

"Mrs. Davenport." Veronica breaks through your daze, gently tugging your sleeve. "What's wrong?"

A long, awkward pause ensues. You're not sure what to say; out of nervousness, you blurt, "I didn't know your parents weren't American."

You hand Veronica a tissue. She wipes her eyes and asks, "What's an American?"

Your mind churns. The morning is passing in a blur. All is not well in your fifth-grade class, Colfax, Nebraska, United States, Earth.

Who Should Be American?

Veronica's situation is not an isolated incident. It's happening all over the United States as officials debate about how to deal with an estimated 11.2 million unauthorized immigrants living in the United States as of March 2010 (Passel & Cohn, 2011). Many of these immigrants have been in the United States long enough to have children who are legal citizens by birth.

"What is an American?" is an innocent question asked by an equally innocent student, and it is not easy to answer. The truth in the United States is often harsh, as the Martinez's all-too-true scenario shows. Technically, anybody living in North, Central, and South America is an American. The term denotes a continent, much as do the words *European* or *Asian*, though in the vernacular, many believe it refers to ethnicity, connoting the sense of peoplehood felt by those living in the United States of America.

By law, anyone born in the United States is a citizen. Immigrants can be naturalized to become citizens. But being a citizen is one thing; being an American is another. What about Native Americans? They immigrated here ten thousand years ago or so and were finally declared citizens of the United States in 1923. Before that, the federal government viewed them as members of separate nations with whom treaties were made. Once on reservations, Native Americans were viewed as wards of the state. When did they become Americans?

As slaves, African Americans were not citizens. They also were not considered persons. The U.S. Supreme Court ruled in the Dred Scott decision of 1857 that people of African descent imported into the United States and held as slaves—and their descendants, slaves or free—were not protected by the Constitution, because slaves were deemed not *persons* under the law and could not be citizens of the United States. In fact, the U.S. Supreme Court declared slaves the property of their owners, much like livestock to be bought and sold at auctions, regardless of family ties. When slavery was dissolved, African Americans finally became persons and citizens under the Thirteenth and Fourteenth Amendments to the U.S. Constitution. However, even after becoming citizens, African and Native Americans were far from "first-class" Americans due to segregation, prejudice, and discrimination. When did they become Americans?

So what do you tell Veronica? What do you tell yourself?

One thing is certain. An American is an immigrant. Native Americans were the first to immigrate to the Americas. Most African Americans were involuntary immigrants, brought in slave ships. The Spanish, English, and French immigrated as colonizers and made their marks. Some came seeking economic opportunity. Others came as refugees fleeing persecution by governments or religions. For principally the same reasons as in the past, many people from all over the world continue to immigrate to the United States.

Americans have always boasted, "We are a nation of immigrants." Sometimes beneath the prideful boast an almost inaudible whisper is heard: "But some immigrants are better than others." A broad sweep of U.S. history shows that ambivalence toward immigrants is endemic in American life. What may have started as concern over culture and language evolved to a concern about culture, language, and race.

Early in the nation's history, one group, which included Benjamin Franklin, worried about the Germanization of the nascent English colonies by German immigrants. They feared German immigrants might outnumber the colonists from the British Isles and compel everyone to speak German. To impede "Germanization," they advocated admission only of English-speaking immigrants from the British Isles. Franklin shared the fear that Germans might crowd out the English-speaking colonists. He did not oppose admission of Germans, but thought it wise to disperse them among the English-speaking colonists to prevent German enclaves from forming (Franklin, 2004).

Franklin and the others feared the Germans would change the culture and language of the British colonists—a fear common among the British settlers. After 1776, the fear of Germans devolved into something broader as the new nation grew to fear anybody who was not British, Protestant, and white. That fear provoked a political party in the middle 1800s. Nicknamed the "Know Nothings," it was officially known as the "American Party." It opposed immigration of Catholics, Jews, and non-whites. The party's followers were termed *nativists* (Knobel, 1996). The nativist attitude rooted firmly in American soil and evolved to what Harvard professor Milton Gordon called the "Anglo-conformity melting pot" (Gordon, 1964).

In this version of the melting pot, America existed for white Anglo-Saxon Protestants (WASPs), and English was the American language. These beliefs were reflected in legislation of the 19th and early 20th centuries that restricted immigration from China and Japan as well from Southern and Eastern Europe; these immigrants were perceived as the "lowest" of whites because of their national origins (Grant, 1970). Quotas and literacy requirements were established favoring Northern and Western Europeans; Southern European cultures and languages were disparaged. Many immigrants changed their names to appear and sound English.

Concurrent to the evolution of the exclusive attitude toward immigrants, an opposite attitude rooted: a more inclusive, pluralistic attitude expressed by another group, which included George Washington (Hing, 2004). This group believed the United States should be a sanctuary for anybody from any nation seeking economic freedom or freedom from oppression. This group's magnanimous attitude also took root in American life and is eloquently expressed in Emma Lazarus's sonnet, "The New Colossus," inscribed at the base of the Statue of Liberty in New York Harbor. The poem declares in part: "Give me your tired, your poor, / your huddled masses yearning to breathe free." This was the national cauldron envisioned by Israel Zangwill in his early 20th century play, *The Melting Pot*, in which the United States was likened to an orchestra of disparate voices, tones, and notes, different ethnicities working and playing together in harmony, melting together as one. Zangwill is credited for coining the term the "melting pot."

Meanwhile, apartheid also took root. Though prejudice against some Southern Europeans eventually slackened, discrimination and segregation remained the lot of African Americans, Asians, Latinos, and Native Americans for many years. The contradiction between professed American ideals of equality and actual American experience became more and more apparent as the United States developed, and it did not dissolve with the Civil War and the end of slavery.

Americans All!

There is hope. The 20th century showed a decisive shift toward inclusion of immigrants and minorities, and the definition of what it means to be an American is also becoming more inclusive. The contradictions are slowly diminishing as society becomes more accepting, with each generation forming its own definition about what it means to be an American.

In 1947, President Harry S. Truman spoke before an audience of the National Association for the Advancement of Colored People (NAACP). He stated his belief about what it means to be an American:

> As Americans we believe every man should be free to live his life as he wishes. He should be limited only by his responsibility to his fellow countrymen. If his freedom is to be more than a dream, each man must be guaranteed equality of opportunity. The only limit to an American's achievement should be his ability, his industry and his character. (Truman, 1965, p. 181)

During the 1950s, a landmark U.S. Supreme Court decision further advanced the shift toward inclusion regarding what it means to be an American. Thurgood Marshall, a young lawyer and president of the NAACP, conceived the idea of a class-action suit, *Brown v. Board of Education of Topeka*. Sponsored by the NAACP, the suit challenged educational segregation in universities, colleges, and public school districts by bringing together five cases: *Brown* itself, *Briggs v. Elliott* (South Carolina), *Davis v. County School Board of Prince Edward County* (Virginia), *Gebhart v. Belton* (Delaware), and *Bolling v. Sharpe* (Washington, DC).

The suit challenged the *Plessy v. Ferguson* doctrine that allowed segregation under the "separate but equal" doctrine. Marshall argued that separate public school, college, and university facilities were inherently unequal, both in fact and their psychological impact. Segregated facilities were poorly funded and dilapidated. Worse, the segregated institutions were nefarious because they created a caste system based on race and a climate of inferiority for minority students. In 1954, the Supreme Court affirmed Marshall's argument that segregation was inherently unequal, thereby quashing the older separate but equal doctrine and beginning the end to *de jure* segregation. (Marshall went on, of course, to become the first African American to serve as a justice on the U.S. Supreme Court, 1967–1991.)

In the late 1950s and early 1960s, Martin Luther King Jr., a young minister and graduate of Harvard University, sought inclusion through unity. He unified grassroots movements into a coalition of men and women from all backgrounds—African Americans, whites, Jews, and so on—and took the cause of inclusion to the American people, culminating in a march on Washington, where more than a million followers congregated on the mall to hear King's speech, "I Have a Dream," delivered in front of the Lincoln Memorial facing the Washington Monument.

The speech was an instant success. It affirmed the idea of equality as expressed in the Declaration of Independence, in President Lincoln's Gettysburg Address, in President Truman's definition of an American, in the *Brown* decision, and restated by King in his speech, paraphrased here: that one day his children would be judged by the quality of their character rather than the color of their skin.

By the 1970s, the idea of the melting pot was critically scrutinized, if not entirely discarded. Even the inclusive melting pot was questioned. Pundits quipped such things as, "minorities had stuck to the bottom of the pot," "minorities had slipped through the pot's crack," or "the melting pot was not intended for people of color." Preeminent scholars questioned the validity of the melting pot for its lack of inclusion, including James Banks, the internationally recognized scholar of multicultural education:

> The elimination of differences among peoples of diverse nationalities was the essence of the "melting pot" concept. . . . While the United States has successfully assimilated groups which share a set of values and behavior patterns of European origin, it has blatantly denied its black, brown, red and yellow citizens the opportunity to fully share in the American dream. (Banks, 1972, p. 266)

Alternative metaphors were proposed to describe American life as inclusive of all peoples, regardless of race, color, religion, class, gender, sexual orientation, and national origins. One metaphor depicted America as a mosaic of people of many shades and colors, another as a kaleidoscope of people of different shapes and sizes.

All the new metaphors strived to describe Americans as different and yet unified, as diverse yet harmonious. The metaphors conveyed ideals of people living in harmony while maintaining their cultural identities. All call for the United States to live up to its own motto, "e pluribus unum," which means "out of many, one." In this union of diverse individuals, the motto suggests, we seek a balance between each individual's rights and the rights of the community as a whole.

By the 1980s, a lively debate about diversity had penetrated the highest levels of civic discourse—a debate that continues today. In political campaigns, candidates now actively seek the votes of women and various ethnic constituencies. Contenders appear before the League of Women Voters, the NAACP, the League of United Latin American Citizens (LULAC), and other groups, courting their support.

The issues of race, gender, sexual orientation, immigration, and poverty prominent during the 2008 presidential campaign led to another historic first, the election of the nation's first African American president,

Barack Obama—who soon after appointed the first Latino female to the U.S. Supreme Court, Sonia Sotomayor.

So who is an American? The diversity of prominent persons such as President Obama and Supreme Court Justice Sotomayor puts a different spin on the question. Like many others, Obama and Sotomayor took advantage of American education and opportunities while still retaining their ethnic heritage. In the new pluralism, we are all free to take the best of our home cultures and meld it with the best of other cultures.

Much work remains to reach the ideal of inclusion. The United States remains an experiment that tests the proposition that a government based on the equality of all of its citizens can prevail for the people, by the people, and of the people. Thus far, the experiment has proved successful, in the main and sometimes in the breach. Some of the questions of the civic discourse have been answered. I believe that sexism and racism have been somewhat reduced, for example, but problems persist: homophobia, religious intolerance, fear of immigrants, and rising poverty in the land of plenty. Yet we must continue to talk, weigh, consider, and act if we wish to continue the shift toward the ideal of inclusion. That is how each generation continues to refine the experiment.

Reflections

This chapter raises two fundamental concerns. First, what does it mean to be a *person*, or a human? Second, what does it mean to be an *American*? Reflect and then discuss these concerns within the context of the following questions:

1. What are Veronica's rights as a human being? To answer this question, examine the United Nations' Universal Declaration of Human Rights.

2. The U.S. government will honor Veronica's rights as a citizen, but should it honor the human rights of her Mexican parents and brothers? If yes, how? If no, why not?

3. Should Veronica assimilate into American society by forsaking her parent's language and culture and adopting American ways and speaking only English? To answer this question, examine the social and political reasons for the development of the Anglo-conformity melting pot, Zangwill's idea of a melting pot, and the proliferation of metaphors during the latter half of the 20th century. How did these metaphors envision an "American"? How did the metaphors treat the cultures and languages of immigrants?

4. Discuss the limitations of a society based on assimilation in which everybody is culturally the same. Discuss the limitations of an integrated society in which everybody is culturally different. Then discuss the advantages of each kind of society.

two

Diversity in a Free Society

We return to Veronica and her question, "What is an American?" The legal answer is easy. The philosophical answer is more difficult because it goes to state of mind, feelings, and allegiance. Those allowed to enter the United States serve to define the American character and will influence what the nation becomes. New arrivals bring their cultures and languages and attempt to preserve the best of their own while adopting the best the United States has to offer. In this chapter, we continue to examine American society by analyzing how 20th century immigration shaped the United States. We then examine the intersection of human diversity and national unity, religious diversity, and their impact on the development of the American educational system.

Shifting Demographics of Immigration

Despite the 20th century shift toward inclusion described in the last chapter, ambivalence toward immigrants persists in subtle and not-so-subtle forms (Murillo, 2002). Some cities create ordinances that forbid landlords to rent to undocumented individuals; elsewhere, illegal vigilante patrols round up people crossing the desert along the Mexican and American borders. This ambivalence is symptomatic of concern about what it means to be an American and who should be considered American.

The faces of immigration have changed since the founding of the United States. During the 20th century, the national origins of immigrants to the United States shifted from largely European nations to Latin American and Asian nations. In his study *Defining America Through Immigration Policy*, Bill Ong Hing (2004) presents volumes of data collected by the INS and the U.S. Census Bureau that show the changing policies and practices of the U.S. government toward immigrants. I have aggregated some of his data in the following paragraphs.

Although the flow of immigrants was and remains constant, during the 20th century, the number of immigrants and their national origins varied not only with U.S. immigration policies, but also according to world conditions, especially wars. There were two peaks. In 1905, 1,350,000 immigrants entered the United States, largely from Europe. In 1990, 1,800,000 entered, largely from Asia, Mexico, and Central and South America. In 2000, 33 percent of the immigrants in the United States were from Mexico and other Central American countries, 25 percent were from Asia, 15 percent from Europe, and the remaining from other parts of the world, including the Middle East (Hing, 2004).

Table 2.1 shows the percentage of immigrants from various parts of the world.

Table 2.1: Percentage of U.S. Immigrants, 1901–1920 and 1981–2000

Origin	1901–1920	1981–2000
Europe	83.4	12.6
Mexico, Central America, and South America	12.0	49.3
Asia	4.0	33.1
Africa	0.1	3.0
Oceania	0.5	2.0

Source: Hing, 2004

The data show a shifting ethnic composition during the 20th century. At the century's dawn, about 84 percent of all immigrants were white Europeans. At its dusk, 87 percent were non-European and non-white.

The United States has undergone a major demographic shift due not only to this trend in immigration, but also to declining birthrates of whites in the 20th century. With that shift comes a concurrent change in the nation's complexion and culture. According to the U.S. Census Bureau, as of 2005 the population has become "majority minority" in four states—California (57 percent), Hawaii (77 percent), New Mexico (56 percent), and Texas (51 percent)—as well as the District of Columbia (70 percent). In these places, non-whites constitute the majority of the population.

Five other states are next in line with a minority population of about 40 percent: Arizona, Georgia, Maryland, Mississippi, and New York (U.S. Census Bureau, 2005). When the 2010 Census data are available, the numbers will no doubt be much larger.

Even our kitchen tables show signs of the demographic shift. According to Karen Collins (2006), reporting on msnbc.com, "Salsa has become a more popular condiment than ketchup, according to some sales reports." That's quite a claim! Next we'll hear that tacos have displaced hot dogs in eating contests.

It is nearly impossible to define ethnically representative American food, be it sushi, barbecued ribs, tacos, hot dogs, or pizzas. This is good. Our foods are rooted in other cultures and yet are still authentically American. Let's not dwell on the salsa claim to gold medal status and keep our taste for the main point—America is changing again and again.

So what is an American? For Veronica, there are no satisfactory answers. She will be separated from her family for long periods during her childhood. It is possible she will never be reunited to live with her family. Even if she returns to Mexico after high school graduation, she may not fit in, or she may like the United States better than Mexico and return.

As educators supporting students like Veronica, we can do much to make her school years easier beyond providing her with an excellent education. Forming support groups of other concerned young people and adults will ensure she has a family of friends. An Internet support system (see chapter 8) can help her keep in touch with family and friends in Mexico between summer and holiday visits. There are many other options possible through her church or other community agencies.

Unifying Beliefs

Even so, there still remains much for Veronica—and for all our students—to learn about what it means to be an American. While it may be difficult, even controversial to attempt to identify core American beliefs, I suggest that there are three unifying beliefs that form the foundation of American education: (1) equality, (2) e pluribus unum (out of many, one), and (3) mutual respect.

Equality

The Preamble to the Declaration of Independence succinctly states the core American belief in equality: "We hold these truths to be self-evident, that all men are created equal, that they are endowed by their Creator with certain inalienable rights, that among these are life, liberty, and the pursuit of happiness." Equality is assumed to be a self-evident truth. We believe all individuals are inherently worthy by virtue of being human.

In 1776 when Thomas Jefferson penned the equality declaration, he was uttering a revolutionary idea about how humans perceive and accept each other. He challenged ancient castes and hierarchies, disrupting long-held beliefs about the nature of humans and their societies. In fact, at the time, women had few rights; masters owned their slaves; the poor had little chance to rise from poverty; the disabled were ostracized, abandoned to atrophy. Today we interpret Jefferson's words to mean that all people are worthy and should have equal rights to live a good life, regardless of social class, race, religion, gender, sexual orientation, and ability.

Out of Many, One

Equality can only be achieved in a community that shares a belief in each individual's inherent worth. E pluribus unum, an expression both of diversity and of unity, captures this sense of individuals coming together as one within a representative republic. The United States and Canada have historically drawn their populations from immigrant peoples of many origins. For both countries, the survival of democracy has required a weaving together of diverse individual histories and cultural heritages into the unifying fabric of nationhood.

Within this national unity, however, individual freedom is preserved. This freedom is the hallmark of democratic societies. Americans and Canadians, for example, exercise a number of freedoms, such as the freedom of religion and the freedom of speech. The essence of these freedoms is the freedom to be different—to hold individual beliefs and to express individual opinions that do not necessarily conform to prevailing or dominant ideas in the society.

This is not to say that there are no societal norms. Unrestrained freedom is chaos. The true value of e pluribus unum rests with the willingness of a nation's citizens to find common ground—and common respect for differences. The common ground, translated into norms of behavior based on rule by law, balances a value of difference, or individuality, with a value of social unity.

Mutual Respect

I would argue that the *unum* (one) of e pluribus unum implies a social contract based on mutual respect for the rights of others. This implicit social contract is a tacit agreement that each one will honor the rights of others so others will return that respect. This civil society founded on the precepts of democracy, therefore, balances the freedom to be different with the obligation to conform to certain norms.

Free societies are naturally discordant, and social order always is a concern. U.S. Supreme Court Justice Oliver Wendell Holmes once characterized free society as messy business. Similarly, institutions based on free expression and free association invariably reverberate with debate and dissension, as individual opinions, needs, and desires clash in the open forum of civic discourse. Such is necessarily the case in the public schools of a democracy.

While dissenters from the prevailing thought stream are not always honored, the citizenry is obligated to tolerate the expression of their ideas. Indeed, new ideas often emerge from dissent to become dominant over time. The growth of a nation is fueled by the untidy interplay and creative tensions of daily life. Nothing is more powerful than an idea whose time has come. In the 1920s the idea whose time had come was women's suffrage; in the 1960s it was black civil rights, and in the 1970s, the civil rights of the disabled. Some would argue that when we look back at the first decades of the 21st century, it will have been the civil rights of homosexuals.

Conflict, therefore, is not merely inevitable. It is necessary. But no society, however free, can allow civil messiness to dissolve the bond of national unity. The glue of social unity—of peoplehood—is civility and mutual respect. For the most part, civility is neither written into law nor expressed as explicit rules. It is an unwritten social contract. Civility is deeply embedded in the folkways and mores of democratic living. It serves as the conflict-resolution mechanism of social order, and it permeates the law without being "the law."

While conflict is inevitable, community is not. As a social contract, it is voluntary to work together, find common ground, and work out our differences. Think of civility as disagreeing in an agreeable way. Conflict should be resolved through discourse and laws, when needed, rather than through violence. The rule of law protects everybody, especially those who are not powerful or strong enough to protect themselves. The rule of law also defines rights and responsibilities, holding unlawful individuals accountable for violations.

Religious Diversity

E pluribus unum describes a delicate balance between pursuit of self or group interests and a willingness to subject oneself to the norms of the greater society, a balance in which neither extreme individualism nor conformity is desirable. The struggle to find this balance can be seen in the history of religious diversity in the United States: its role in the founding of the United States and of the American education system, and its continuing status in education as an area of tension between honoring diversity and supporting unity.

The Road to the First Amendment

The pre-Revolutionary War was an era of people seeking religious freedom, from Puritans in the Massachusetts Bay Colony, to Quakers and Amish in Pennsylvania, to Roman Catholics in Maryland, to Dutch Reformed in New York, and to Anglicans and Baptists in the Southern colonies. By the time the U.S. Constitution was adopted, Scandinavian and German Lutherans, German Catholics, Scotch-Irish Protestants, French Catholics, and Jews had settled villages and farming areas or established neighborhoods identifiable by churches and synagogues in such cities as New York, Boston, and Philadelphia.

By the time the Constitution was ratified, religious pluralism was a fact of American communal life.

This is not to say there was no conflict between the various groups. There was plenty. For example, some of the colonies required membership in a specific Christian denomination, if one was to be a fully certified citizen, and some religious leaders attempted to dictate government policies. This led to the enactment of the first amendment of the Bill of Rights, which disallows religion as a test of citizenship, separates church and state, and recognizes religious pluralism. Thomas Jefferson, as the architect of separation of church and state, saw the need for a unifying ethical structure to guide a democratic nation that had no established religious creed:

> The interests of society require the observation of those moral precepts only in which all religions agree . . . (for all forbid us to murder, plunder, and steal, or bear false witness) and that we should not intermeddle with the particular dogmas in which all religions differ. (as cited in Padover, 1939, p. 116)

Separation of church and state thus requires the state to function on ethics universal to all religions, and not to meddle, in Jefferson's words, "with the particular dogmas in which all religions differ."

The separation doctrine created a binary social structure for communal life. It apportioned morals and ethics between the church and state, with the church appropriating the private sector of living, and the state the public sector. In our private lives, we can do and believe whatever we wish. In public, we are bound by the ethics of civility—equality and mutual respect—echoed in the Declaration of Independence and the Constitution. The First Amendment provided all citizens freedom of conscience (the free exercise thereof) and freedom from an established church: "Congress shall make no law respecting an establishment of religion, or prohibiting the free exercise thereof" (Legal Information Institute, n.d.). In other words, religious freedom was an individual right to *and* from religion.

The State of Religious Pluralism

Numerous conflicts have challenged religious pluralism and the First Amendment. Yet religious pluralism has prevailed, mainly because it enables government and church to develop vigorously and independently.

Today, multiple faith communities thrive in the United States, communities that are often ethnically and linguistically diverse within a common religion.

According to the *World Christian Encyclopedia* (Barrett, Kurian, & Johnson, 2001), Christianity is the United States' largest religion, but there are many other active religions (see table 2.2). While these data are more than ten years old, in my judgment they still reflect the proportional relationship between religions in the United States. In another ten years, it is possible that the proportions will change. The data illustrate religious pluralism. It is extremely difficult to find up-to-date data on the demography of world religions, because no neutral collection agencies exist for such information. Throughout this section, I am relying mainly on data published by Oxford University Press, because of the press's reputation for integrity.

Table 2.2: Religion in the United States in 2001

Religion	Number of U.S. Adherents	Percentage of U.S. Population
Christianity	160,000,000	77
Judaism	2,832,000	1.3
Islam	1,104,000	0.5
Buddhism	1,082,000	0.5
Hinduism	766,000	0.4
Unitarian	629,000	0.3
Wicca	307,000	0.1
Spiritualism	116,000	0.05
Native American	103,000	0.05
Baha'i	84,000	0.04

Source: Barrett, Kurian, & Johnson, 2001, p. 170

Outside of those listed in table 2.2, other faith communities exist as well. Furthermore, many faiths are diverse in themselves, containing various denominations, sects, and variations. According to the *Yearbook of American and Canadian Churches* (Lindner, 2009), there are at least twenty-five different Christian denominations in the United States, in addition to faith communities not reporting information to the yearbook.

Religious diversity in Canada is equally robust. About 80 percent of Canadians are Christians; Christianity has at least eighty-one distinct denominations (Lindner, 2009). See table 2.3 for the six largest denominations in order of membership.

Table 2.3: Largest Canadian Christian Denominations

Denomination	Number of Adherents
Roman Catholic Church—Canada	12,987,637
United Church of Canada	1,358,000
Greek Orthodox	350,000
Presbyterian Church—Canada	181,400
Church of Latter Day Saints	178,100
Evangelical Lutheran Church	174,555

Source: Lindner, 2009, pp. 358–362

Of course, there are other active non-Christian religious communities in Canada, such as Chinese Folk Religionists, Jews, Muslims, Hindus, Sikhs, and Buddhists. For context, see table 2.4 (page 24), which lists the world's ten largest religions—the third-largest group claims no religion—in descending order by numbers and percentage of world population.

Complete figures on religious adherents are difficult to collect. All of the previous figures on U.S., Canadian, and world religions are based on the best available statistical analysis. There is a margin of error due to differences in resources and cultures. For example, Islam may be the largest religion in the world, but definitions of *adherents* differ worldwide. In other words, collecting a totally accurate count of the adherents to the many religions is not a precise science.

Table 2.4: World's Ten Largest Religions in 2001

Religion	Number of Adherents	Percentage of World Population
Christianity	2.1 billion	33%
Islam	1.5 billion	21%
Nonreligious	1.1 billion	16%
Hinduism	900 million	14%
Indigenous/tribal	375 million	6%
Buddhism	375 million	6%
Chinese traditional	375 million	6%
African traditional	100 million	2%
Judaism	14 million	.25%
Baha'i	7 million	.12 %

Source: Lindner, 2009

Religion in Early American Education

The impact of the First Amendment on education is long standing. There were difficulties among religious groups before and after the amendment's guarantee, and it took a while before religious and political leaders supported it.

In fact, early education was often deeply interwoven with religious education, which was itself interwoven with notions of national identity. In the early 1600s, Spanish missionaries made an effort to win over Mexican Indians by using their native languages to convert them (thus introducing bilingual education). The intent was to use materials translated in the pupil's native language while also teaching a new second language. Once the second language was learned, the first would no longer be used. Franciscan priests recorded the dialects of various tribes and composed bilingual texts to teach Spanish Catholicism. One extant book, Francisco Pareja's (1613) *Confessional in the Castilian and Timuquana Languages,* was written in Timuquana and Spanish. Its text and artwork depicted the tribe's customs and rituals as immoral from a Christian viewpoint and allowed the missionaries to enter the Indians' cultures in an effort to stamp out their religious beliefs and practices and replace them with Christianity. In this case, education served the purpose of religious conversion. Similarly, both Protestant and Catholic faiths imposed their respective denominations on Native American students for many years, starting in the late 1800s and ending in the 1950s. The Bureau of Indian Affairs (BIA) boarding schools hired missionary teachers and administrators to use Christianity to "Americanize" the students.

The English colonists were also keen on education for religious purposes, with aim on salvation rather than conversion. In the Massachusetts Bay Colony, Puritan leaders passed a law called the "Old Deluder Satan Act." The law required parents to educate their children in the Puritan religion so the children would know how to evade Satan and live a good life—that is, conduct themselves as Puritans. The law required the children to learn to read English to be able to understand the Bible and other Puritan scriptures.

The Puritans instituted the use of a basal primer (often bilingual; by 1775, at least 118 German/English bilingual schools existed for the religious education of Lutheran children, as well as seminaries to prepare teachers). The primer was designed to teach English spelling, pronunciation, punctuation, and grammar, thereby preparing pupils to read original literature—mostly religious in this case. The *New England Primer* contained the Lord's Prayer and the Puritan Catechism—a didactic dialogue between Christ, the Devil, and youth, which the children recited as a play.

By 1844 in Philadelphia, religious lessons were taught in public schools, as approved by state law. Some Philadelphia Protestants insisted on religious lessons by using the King James Bible. When a teacher introduced the Roman Catholic's Douay-Rheims version into her classes, the Protestants rioted in the Catholic neighborhoods, burning Catholic churches and homes (Johnson, 1973).

Religion in Education in the Modern Era

Debates over the role of religion in education continued in the 20th century. My research found that during the 1920s, Christian fundamentalists successfully campaigned for laws prohibiting the teaching of evolution in the notorious 1925 "Scopes Monkey Trial." In the 1970s, Christian fundamentalists again campaigned against the theory of evolution. Rather than taking an anti-evolution stance, as did the earlier fundamentalists, they conducted a pro-knowledge campaign: they proposed that what they termed "creation science" should be given equal time with the theory of evolution in public school science classes. Creation science is the belief that an omniscient being created all living forms as they currently exist and as described in the Old Testament's Genesis. As such, it contradicts the evolution theory that all living forms emerged from simpler forms. When the U.S. Supreme Court ruled various times during the 1980s that creation science could not be taught as a science, creationists reformulated their idea as "intelligent design." This is the belief that the universe—and all living things—are best explained as the result of an intelligent cause that created everything from nothing, and not by an indirect process, such as Darwin's natural selection. The intelligent design reformulation avoided specifying the nature or identity of the designer. As of yet, few (if any) states—to my knowledge—have adopted intelligent design to be taught in their schools as an alternate scientific theory of the creation of the universe and all living things.

Respecting Religious Diversity in Education

"As long as you give tests," some of my students used to joke, "there will be prayers in school!" We all chuckled, but that is the way it should be. Students should be free to pray when they wish. That is their right, so long as their prayers do not interfere with the other students and their rights of freedom to religion, and freedom from religion.

Keep in mind all individuals in public schools have freedom to and from religion. Students and teachers do not surrender any of their constitutional rights in public schools, including the right to believe and worship as they please. In school, students and teachers may pray, meditate, and wear religious objects and clothing, as they desire. Yet they must respect the rights of others.

Let's examine the topic further with a couple of illustrations. Some expressions of religion—such as active proselytizing or preaching—can be intrusive in the school setting and should not be allowed. Most expressions, however, are not. Religious symbols—such as wearing a crucifix or a Star of David on a necklace, a yarmulke on the head, or ashes on the forehead on Ash Wednesday—need not be intrusive. In fact, these nonintrusive examples are sufficiently common in American and Canadian society that they should be well known by teachers. Asking Catholic children to wash their "dirty" foreheads on Ash Wednesday—this has been known to happen—trammels benign religious expression and is unnecessary and indeed unconstitutional. Nonacceptance in this form singles out students who are different from others and can be both harassing and alienating.

While Jewish, Catholic, and Protestant religious customs and symbols are fairly well known in the United States and Canada, religious customs and symbols from non-Western cultures are less well known. In some Southeast Asian religions, for example, the head is considered to be a sacred temple. To pat someone on the head is a violation of the sacred temple, an act of desecration. While the approving, affectionate patting of children's heads is a common, accepted practice in Western societies, it is a gesture reserved for parents (if for anyone) in certain Asian societies. When a teacher pats an Asian student on the head, that gesture, however well meaning, may be interpreted as offensive.

Teachers simply have to know the cultures of their students. The previous example is only one of many that might occur in the classroom. Teachers cannot be expected to know the many existent religious observations or practices, but they can be expected to remain alert to their students' action and reactions. It never hurts to discreetly ask them or their parents about religious preferences and practices.

While it is challenging to learn about the many different religious faiths in the world, teachers can familiarize themselves in general terms with many of the major religions, such as animism, Buddhism, Christianity, Hinduism, Islam, and Judaism. In learning about these religions, I have found it useful to study the historical development of each and its basic beliefs or doctrines. Religion intertwines with culture when religion-based practices become associated with particular cultures, but that does not mean that everyone in that culture adheres to the primary religion's strictures. Individual differences must be taken into account and yet treated with respect, because in childhood, particularly, any difference can be magnified into a reason for teasing, shunning, or abusing.

Religious differences are factors of student diversity. How teachers respond to those differences affects how students and their parents understand and feel about the school experience. Culture and religion intertwine, which may complicate matters and give rise to stereotypes. Yet religious differences among students can be fertile ground for learning.

Of course, under various Supreme Court rulings, schools may not foster or promote any particular religion. This includes administrative decisions and teaching decisions. For example, schools may not allow holidays for Christians only; Christmas pageants, once a standard in elementary schools, must now be more eclectic, including songs and skits of non-Christian faiths. The separation of church and state doctrine applies to schools because taxpayers' money from the local, state, and federal levels funds public schools. Schools are state agencies; teachers act as agents of the state and thus cannot sponsor or promote religious practices.

However, religion need not be a controversial subject in public schools. The Supreme Court allows schools to teach about different religions in literature, history, geography, and other classes where religion is a part of the lesson's content. For example, in literature classes, excerpts from the Koran, the Torah, the Bible, and the sacred texts of other religions can be studied. In history and geography classes, events such as large-scale human migrations or wars can be viewed from religious as well as economic and political perspectives.

Some high schools now offer an elective in world religions. One high school in Modesto, California, requires a world religion course for all seniors because of the religious diversity of its community. The course is not a requirement promoting religion. Rather, the course fosters global awareness of cultural diversity through the lens of world religions. Because religion and culture intertwine, it makes good sense to teach about the religions reflected in history, literature, art, language, and music. When possible, clergy and others knowledgeable about different religions should be invited to class to explain their faith. Parents should be informed of the speaker and contents of the speech, and if wanted, they can request an alternative experience for their children. The presentation should be incorporated into the lesson's continuum and students should be prepared beforehand with information about the faith, which may be procured from the invited speaker.

Conclusion

Educators are becoming increasingly aware of and interested in diversity issues. Much has been made in the media of North America's increasing "diversity." I use quotation marks because the populations of both Canada and the United States, both nations of immigrants, have always been diverse. But *recognition* of such diversity is of more recent origin, brought about in part by population increases among minorities.

Canada has perhaps used more specific official language to recognize diversity than has the United States. A bill passed by the Canadian House of Commons in 1988, for example, states:

> It is hereby declared to be the policy of the Government of Canada to recognize and promote the understanding that multiculturalism reflects the cultural and racial diversity of Canadian society and acknowledges the freedom of all members of Canadian society to preserve, enhance, and share their cultural heritage. (Canadian Multiculturalism Act, 1985)

Some would argue that such a policy is implicit in the United States, at least in certain areas, although nativism and the Anglo-conformity melting pot militate against diversity. Others would point to wide disparities in philosophies of preserving, enhancing, and sharing cultural heritages. To teach about diversity in a positive way and to help children value rather than denigrate difference, teachers and administrators should acknowledge the diversity around them and respond to it. Sensitivity to diversity can help teachers adopt approaches that make it possible for all children to realize their potential.

Reflections

People often take their values and folkways for granted and cannot explain the rationale undergirding them. Research, reflect on, and discuss the following questions about American core values.

1. The Declaration of Independence and the U.S. Constitution, including its Bill of Rights, are based on two principles, the equality of all humans and the rule of law. What is meant by these principles? Where did they come from? Do research on the Magna Carta and other English bills of rights. Also examine the Enlightenment, especially the writings of John Locke on government and Jean-Jacques Rousseau on the social contract. Then report your findings in an essay, or conduct a group discussion based on your findings.

2. Religious pluralism is a solid value and reality in American communal life. Research and report on the religious pluralism of your community, campus, or area. Try to understand the reasons for the pluralism. If the area is religiously homogeneous, try to determine why. Be careful with hasty conclusions. For example, a farming area may appear to be mainly Lutheran until you look more closely and discover Lutherans are not all the same: their congregations differ by synod association. Similarly, in my town of Lincoln, Nebraska, there is a large community of Vietnamese people adhering to various Buddhist, Catholic, and other faiths.

3. Research the topic of bilingual education in the United States to identify its many uses, such as religious indoctrination, maintenance of a student's home language and culture, or as a transitional approach while the student is learning English. Consider answering such questions as: should schools use bilingual instruction to maintain the student's home language?

4. Research the topic of assimilation of American Indians via the U.S. government's Bureau of Indian Affairs boarding schools. Describe the policy's original purpose, how it was implemented, and why it ceased in the 1970s.

5. Consider the various approaches that can be used to accommo-
    date non-English speaking students to learn English. Research
    what experts say are the strengths and limitations of the various
    approaches.

Stand and Deliver

We live in dynamic times. Teachers must be intellectually dynamic, and
they must help students realize a similar dynamism. You are challenged
to stand and deliver, an exercise in critical thinking. Reflect on, discuss,
weigh, and consider the event. Then, using the key concepts of the
chapter, address the questions posed after the scenario.

Religious differences in the classroom need not be challenging, but
when teachers let down their guards and treat the differences poorly,
bad things happen to well-meaning teachers. The following incident
occurred in the 1960s before teachers had the benefit of exercises
such as this one to reflect on how to manage religious differences in
the classroom. Furthermore, in this case, the parents did not have a
positive attitude toward schools and teachers. They had attended a
Bureau of Indian Affairs boarding school and had a negative experience. They had been punished, much like Juanita, for exhibiting their
cultural and religious beliefs and for speaking their home language.
They did not trust teachers.

Juanita's Dirty Arm

Teachers at a reservation school had been told to respect the culture
of their Native American students, but were taught little about the students' specific tribal culture. One day in a seventh-grade classroom,
the teacher, Mrs. Fonda, noticed that Juanita, normally a tidy youngster, had a brown smear of dirt on one arm. That day and the next,
Mrs. Fonda said nothing about the smear, but when Juanita came a
third day with the smear, Mrs. Fonda could not be silent.

"Juanita, go wash your dirty arm," she said.

"It's not dirty," responded Juanita.

"It looks dirty to me."

"But I've got to . . ." Juanita started to say.

"Don't argue with me," interrupted Mrs. Fonda sternly. "I'm the teacher here. Do what you're told!"

Juanita left the classroom mumbling, but she complied with Mrs. Fonda's command. Two days later, Juanita's parents took her out of school to attend the funeral of her sister. After two weeks she had not returned, and so the principal visited her home to ask why.

Juanita's mother said, "In our way, when someone in the family is ill, each of us places a spot of oil and soil somewhere on our body. We are one with nature. Illness is a sign that we are out of balance with nature. We use the oil and soil of our mother, the Earth, to show that we wish our sick one to be in balance with nature.

"When the teacher made Juanita wash her arm, she broke our one-ness with nature. That is why her sister died. The teacher caused her death. She is bad for Juanita and for our family. Juanita cannot go back to class with Mrs. Fonda."

Questions

1. Describe how you would feel if your teacher forced you to disobey a religious conviction that you believed led to the cause of your sister's death.

2. Consider the scenario from Mrs. Fonda's perspective. Perhaps Mrs. Fonda believed that cleanliness was next to godliness. In other words, she may have been acting from a religious belief herself. Perhaps she was thinking of Juanita's personal hygiene, or she may have thought Juanita was being neglected at home.

3. Now consider the ethical and legal implications of the incident. What responsibility does the school district have toward the teachers? Should Mrs. Fonda have been told about the practice?

4. What is the teacher's responsibility? What responsibility did Mrs. Fonda have for knowing about the religious significance of

the brown smear? Should teachers be experts on all religious symbolism? How should teachers deal with symbolism they don't understand or recognize?

5. What are the parents' responsibilities to Juanita, and how can the principal and teacher help? How can the principal and teacher assist the parents? Remember, the parents do not trust teachers, principals, and schools in general because of their own experience in BIA boarding schools.

three

Universal Education for a Free Society

Prior to the formation of the United States, and for a while afterward, education was a privilege for the wealthy who could afford to hire teachers to instruct their youth. Today publicly funded K–12 schooling is provided for all. Education is an absolute necessity for a democratic, free society, and a state-controlled public education is the epitome of a democracy. The citizens as a community pool their taxes and revenues to fund the schools. The citizens also elect the officials who manage the schools and set curriculum and teaching standards without intervention of the federal government, except in the instances when the state system is not in compliance with the U.S. Constitution, which government agencies must comply with to provide equal protection of the law to all citizens. (See chapter 6 for a discussion about the policy of equal educational opportunity). In broad strokes, this chapter explores the establishment of universal public education in the United States, its rationale, and its goals.

Education for Democracy

Soon after the United States was formed, Thomas Jefferson wrote, "If a nation expects to be ignorant and free, in a state of civilization, it expects what never was and never will be" (as cited in Padover, 1939, p. 89). Jefferson was aware that illiterate and ignorant citizens could not govern themselves and would be ruled instead by the wealthy, who had the money to educate their children. Without public education, the new American government would not be a democracy, but an oligarchy—rule by the few. Democracy and education are thus inextricably linked—addressing the *pluribus* in e pluribus unum—and education for democracy must prepare students to be good citizens.

Jefferson envisioned universal, nonreligious education available for all to ensure the nation would have literate and politically active citizens.

He first attempted to institute this kind of education on a smaller scale in Virginia, where he proposed "A Bill for the More General Diffusion of Knowledge" (Padover, 1939, p. 89). The bill divided Virginia into twenty-four districts subdivided into wards, similar to contemporary counties with school districts. In each, an elementary school was to be built and maintained at the expense of the citizens in the ward. The curriculum consisted of reading, writing, and arithmetic. All free children in the ward, male and female, would receive three years of instruction free of expense, and additional years as their parents chose to pay for it.

In each district, an academy or grammar school was to be established and supported at the public expense to teach the classics, grammar, geography, and the higher branches of arithmetic. Furthermore, district citizens would elect a board of education. The board would hire a superintendent who would hire and evaluate teachers by testing the children. The teacher was retained if the children could recite the knowledge contained in the county board's curriculum.

The bill was not enacted in its original form or in its 1797 revision. Wealthy Virginia citizens did not want to pay taxes for the education of the poor. Though the bill was killed, the idea lived and influenced others. Jefferson's idea laid the conceptual frame for what we have today: publicly funded education. Now some two hundred years later, there are fifty robust school "systems" in the United States, one for each state, under the control of publically elected officials at the district, county, and state levels. One person influenced by Jefferson's ideas was Horace Mann, a U.S. senator from Massachusetts and an advocate of publicly funded schools (Downs, 1974). By the 1840s, the nation was slowly drifting toward industrialization. Large numbers of children lived in cities and were not being educated because they were working in sweatshops, cottage industries, factories, and mills. For numerous reasons, rural areas were slow in establishing schools. A scarcity of teachers existed everywhere, and those who taught were not well trained to teach children. Jefferson's ideal of a literate, politically active citizenship was floundering.

When Mann was appointed to be the superintendent of education for the Massachusetts Board of Education in 1837, he initiated an effort to address the following six theses:

1. People should not remain ignorant, or they will lose their freedom.

2. Publicly funded education should be provided, controlled, and maintained by the public.

3. This kind of education is best when children of all backgrounds attend.

4. This education should be nonsectarian but friendly toward religion.

5. Its philosophy, methods, and values should be those of a free society.

6. Its teachers should be well-trained professionals. (Downs, 1974)

Mann worked tirelessly for a "normal" (ideal or model) school system in Massachusetts. These schools would serve all children as the great equalizer, making the poor equal to others. This education would thus be of practical benefit to the individual as well as the state.

In Mann's vision, children would attend a well-equipped, publicly funded school where they would share a common curriculum and learn the same subjects. Well-trained teachers were the key to make the idea flourish, so Mann established the first normal school for the professional education of teachers. With Mann's assistance, New York State followed Massachusetts's example. By slow degrees, the idea caught on all over the United States. An education was soon considered so important that it became compulsory, which took children out of the labor force where they were being exploited as low-paid workers in mines, mills, and factories.

The term *common schools* flowered nationwide. Schools became the United States' commons, the place the people of a community share for the benefit of the community. There were glitches, however. Because the common schools reflected their communities, they were often segregated by race and class, and in the case of Native Americans, the federal government imposed segregated education in boarding schools far from the student's home reservation. (These are now closed or under Native American control.)

But to this day, schools serve as the commons or center of many communities. Jefferson's ideal—a literate, politically active citizenry—also survives. His ideal has been transformed so that current education serves a trinity of purposes: (1) instruction of the mind with mathematics, sciences, and languages; (2) instruction of the heart with the arts and humanities; and (3) instruction of the body with health and physical education. American public education is often credited for the United States' large middle class and dynamic economy, though both have ups and downs. (Later chapters will discuss whether we have achieved truly universal education; that is, questions of equal access and equal benefit complicate the mere offering of universal education.) It is with those ups and downs in mind we turn to education for freedom.

Education for Freedom

In addition to preparing students to become citizens, education must also prepare them for independent living—the *unum* part of e pluribus unum—to pursue their individual and group interests within the broader parameters of the democratic society. Education for freedom enables individuals to maximize on the opportunities freedom provides.

Individuals must take control of their actions if they desire a good life, which they must also define. After all, the best part of democracy is freedom: you can live as you want. The worst part of democracy is also freedom: nobody will live for you. You are responsible for what you do. We all need help handling freedom.

When we are young, if we have the luck of good parents and other mentors to assist us, we learn to be independent and to take charge of our lives. Yet parents and other mentors are limited by their time, backgrounds, and knowledge for successful living in the increasingly sophisticated, interconnected world of the 21st century.

Public education assists by going beyond education for democracy. Citizenship education is not enough in such a complex world, especially when economies are globally interdependent. Citizens are now members of a global village, and enlightened activism is possible when they are taught to think and do for themselves. In the words of philosopher John Dewey, "The only freedom that is of enduring importance is freedom of intelligence . . . freedom of observation and of judgment exercised on behalf of purposes that are intrinsically worthwhile" (1938, p. 69).

Freedom of intelligence is the freedom to think, feel, and behave in ways that enable individuals to achieve the hopes and dreams that they hold dear—to be happy as long as their aspirations do not trammel the individual freedoms of others. Yet conflict may arise. Here is an example.

How does the language of instruction affect individual freedom as balanced against a societal norm? In chapter 2, bilingual education is described as a tool of oppression as used by Spanish missionaries in Mexico in the 17th century. In chapter 4, bilingual education is described as a tool for providing equal access to knowledge as used in Florida schools for Cuban refugees in the 1960s. Through happenstance, it is possible that bilingual education could result in both oppression and equal access. In Canada, the 1982 Charter of Rights and Freedoms guarantees English-speaking and French-speaking parents that their children can be instructed in either official language. Each Canadian province may apply the bilingual policy as it sees fit in order to serve its citizens. However, in Quebec schools, children are *required* to be educated in French. This practice has antagonized some parents—especially immigrant parents—who, according to their interpretation of the charter, should be allowed to choose either French or English as the language for their children's schooling.

Some would argue that the language policy in Quebec restricts (or at least affects) freedom of intelligence and runs counter to Canada's overall policies of multiculturalism. It allows a dominant language (French) to be an exclusive language—tacitly excluding nonspeakers. The Quebec policy thereby may limit access to learning by non-French-speaking students. According to the national philosophy, Canadian schools in all provinces should work to enhance the cultural traditions of all groups, including new immigrants, regardless of their language. But as of this writing, the tension between Canada's aspirations as a multicultural nation and Quebec's adherence to a French-language schooling tradition has not been resolved to everybody's satisfaction. Individual freedom and a societal norm are out of balance.

The much debated issue of whether bilingual education is good or bad for English learners (ELs) is a misdirected question with a wishy-washy answer: Yes. No. Maybe so. Keep in mind, there is no one right way to teach any group of students. Consequently, one must consider whether bilingual education will benefit a specific student. Then assessments must be conducted to determine whether bilingual education and the particular students are a good match. Teachers should be aware of bilingual education issues, as described in chapter 5.

The Canadian issue on bilingual education described previously is an example of a society striving to find the balance point on fractious issues in which concerned individuals have a legitimate stake in the outcome. Educators are challenged not only to comprehend the issues, but to attend to the various viewpoints, both individual and societal, and then respond in ways that affirm the values of freedom, unity, and civility.

Developing Viable Individuals

As we have seen, education for democracy focuses on the intellectual development of literate and politically active citizens, and education for freedom focuses on the intellectual development of people to pursue meaningful lives, as defined by the individuals themselves. Citizens in a democracy have a need for an education and the reciprocal obligation to become educated. In fact, the U.S. government's contemporary policies of accountability, as in the No Child Left Behind Act's requirements of benchmarks and testing, shift the focus from students "can learn" to students "must learn." Schools and individuals share responsibility for learning. Universal education—comprehensive, global, and multifaceted education available to all youth—can accomplish education for both democracy and freedom.

The purpose of universal education is to assist youth in their development as viable individuals—individuals who are capable of sustaining a good life and of growing and developing spiritually, emotionally, and mentally. *Viable* shares roots with such words as *vivacious* and *vital*, which refer to potency, energy, and spirit. When young people graduate from high school, they should be viable enough to commence an independent life, free to pursue goals intrinsically worthwhile.

Free societies need viable individuals who can think independently and understand the perplexities of the modern world. They should be able to direct their own behavior, respect the rights of others, and function effectively in an interdependent world. Various scholars have explored the idea of viability, but here we will confine ourselves to discussing the work of John Dewey (1859–1952) and three other exemplary scholars who shaped the American education system: W. E. B. Du Bois (1868–1963), George I. Sanchez (1906–1972), and Jane Addams (1860–1935).

John Dewey

John Dewey turned attention to education for freedom during the first decades of the 20th century, when public schools were fast becoming vocational as a result of industrialization and the growing need for factory workers. In the schools, a two-track system was developing. On one track, a liberal arts curriculum for middle- and upper-class students enabled them to pursue professions requiring college and university degrees. On the second track, an industrial curriculum for lower-class students enabled them to enter the labor force without further education. At the time, the lower class was comprised largely of Southeast European immigrants and people of color. Similar industrial boarding schools were established to assimilate Native Americans as farmers and industrial workers. Overall, the industrial schools emulated factories, stressing the efficient mass production of students as commodities prepared to serve business and industry.

Schools as model factories mirrored the nation's social class hierarchy. The first track prepared upper- and middle-class students for white-collar occupations and professions. The second industrial track, composed of lower-class whites and people of color, prepared students to be workers for the white-collar professionals.

A chorus of other school reformers joined Dewey to oppose the outcome of industrial mass education by advocating that schools should prepare viable individuals regardless of class, race, or sex. The purpose of schools, they argued, was to provide students with the intellectual skills and cultural values by which they could think and do for themselves; that is, upon graduation, they could select a particular vocation or profession to pursue, rather than be tracked into one, as with industrial education.

W. E. B. Du Bois

W. E. B. Du Bois was one such reformer. A pioneer in the struggle for the integration of African Americans, Du Bois was opposed to industrial education programs for African Americans because such programs served to limit an individual's education and life choices to narrowly conceived industrial crafts.

The industrial education movement for African Americans taught self-sufficiency, but only through servility as a worker. Such education trained African Americans (men principally) only to be good workers and followers. It did not expose them to the larger world of ideas or prepare them to be leaders. To Du Bois, industrial education prepared African Americans for inferiority (Du Bois, 1903).

Du Bois was a scholar in his own right. Like many intellectuals, he loved the cultural milieu of Paris and European literature, especially William Shakespeare's writings. His opposition to industrial education was founded on a love of all knowledge, and he felt African Americans should be exposed to the world of ideas rather than be restricted to the information needed to pursue a narrow trade.

At a time when the 1896 *Plessy v. Ferguson* doctrine of separate but equal was in full force in many school systems, Du Bois sought education for viability for African Americans, through opportunities equal to those of whites in equitably funded, desegregated schools. As one of the founders of the NAACP, along with people such as James Weldon Johnson and Moorfield Storey, Du Bois worked through that organization to lobby for court decisions supportive of integrated education that would provide equal educational opportunities. He lived long enough to witness the landmark U.S. Supreme Court decision *Brown v. Board of Education* in 1954, which began the dismantling of school segregation in the United States.

George I. Sanchez

George I. Sanchez devoted his life's work to the economic, political, and education problems of Mexican Americans in the Southwest, especially in Texas and New Mexico, where Latinos had lived since the late 16th century. In spite of that long history, Latinos were, to use Sanchez's words, "strangers in their own land, a forgotten people" (Sanchez, 1940, p. 1).

Political corruption and greed deprived Mexican Americans of their land base and economic sustenance, making them second-class citizens. To Sanchez, education was the only permanent solution to the problem. Like Du Bois, he opposed narrowly focused education like the community education experiments in New Mexico that aimed at providing Latino students with skills to be successful only in their own villages. Merely producing contented villagers was a poor goal in Sanchez's eyes. Instead, he favored the kind of education that would prepare Mexican American students to live and to be successful beyond their villages, or if they chose to remain in their villages, to transform them, bringing them into the modern world: "He [the Mexican American] must learn to compete in his society more effectively, he must develop business acumen and learn economic values and he must be fitted to change his society both economically and culturally" (Sanchez, 1940, p. 81).

Sanchez's critics argued that Mexican Americans could not benefit from such education because they were inherently inferior to non-Latinos and therefore incapable of self-determination. As proof, his critics cited Mexican American students' low intelligence quotient (IQ) scores. Sanchez showed that the IQ tests were culturally biased and, for many Spanish-speaking youngsters, virtually unintelligible (Murillo, 1996).

Sanchez opposed the "cognitive deficit" notion that non-whites were inherently less intelligent than whites. He proposed bilingual-bicultural instruction in Spanish and English in the early grades to help Mexican American students make the transition to an English-based curriculum. He believed that a bicultural curriculum would better prepare Mexican Americans to live in their cultural community and in the larger, predominantly white communities. Like W. E. B. Du Bois, Sanchez loved knowledge and was concerned about the intellectual development of Mexican Americans; he wanted them to be introduced to the world of ideas. (Read more about bilingual education and cognitive deficit in chapter 6.)

In the 1940s, Sanchez worked with other Mexican Americans to revitalize a self-help association, the League of United Latin American Citizens. The association's goals were to promote equal education opportunities for Mexican Americans and to provide scholarships for college-bound students. He lived to see bilingual-bicultural education become a reality throughout much of the Southwest with the enactment of various state laws and with support from Title VII of the Elementary and Secondary Education Act of 1965 (Murillo, 1996). For a contemporary assessment of the educational status of Mexican American and other Latinos, see Gándara and Contreras's book *The Latino Education Crisis* (2009).

Jane Addams

Jane Addams devoted her career, from the early 1900s till her death in 1935, to the betterment of European immigrants. She focused on the viability of individuals through her work at a settlement house she established for immigrants in Chicago. Addams worked to ease the strife of assimilation into American life during a time when Southern and Eastern European immigrants lived in poverty and were often exploited in the workplace. She situated the house in the center of Chicago's Greek, German, Jewish, Irish, Italian, and French Canadian neighborhoods.

With her own funds—and assistance from others—Addams developed a comprehensive education program, which became known as Hull House. At its pinnacle, the program hosted two thousand people a week to partake in opportunities such as night school for adults, kindergarten classes, a public kitchen, coffeehouse, library, gymnasium, bathhouse, music school, bookbindery, and drama and other clubs. Hull House's wide array of services and opportunities assisted the immigrant populations surrounding it and eventually became a thirteen-building settlement with a playground and a summer camp. It also served as a model for the development of kindergarten, continuing education for adults, and a training center for the education of social workers. It was widely emulated in cities throughout the United States.

Addams was a social reformer and was active in many causes for the rights of women, African Americans, and Southern and Eastern

European immigrants, especially in the arena of labor unions and child labor laws. Furthermore, she was a first-rate scholar whose publications shaped the paradigm still used for the education of social workers and other human service providers. She was also a stalwart advocate for pacificism, drawing international attention to her humanitarian work for which she was awarded the Nobel Prize in 1931; she was one of the first women to receive the award.

Although Du Bois, Sanchez, and Addams dealt with varied cultural issues, at the heart of their work was the common theme to assist marginalized people to achieve viability through education. They worked against prevailing tides of prejudice and indifference that entrapped immigrant and minority individuals. Their goal was to achieve truly universal education—schooling that was culturally sensitive, that expanded rather than constricted the students' world, and that was as accessible to minorities and immigrants as it was to individuals in the dominant culture.

Universal education is by definition emancipatory. It frees individuals from the constraints of ignorance, a common enemy to all people of all cultures. Mortimer Adler succinctly defines universal education in *The Paideia Proposal*:

> [As] we recognize that twelve years of general, nonspecialized schooling for all is the best policy—the most practical preparation for work— we should all realize that is not its sole justification. It is not only the most expedient kind of schooling, but it is also best . . . because it prepares our children to be good citizens and to lead good human lives. (1982, p. 20)

Notice what Adler does not say. He does not say that schools should teach a student an occupation. In fact, the entire *Paideia Proposal* is based on the assumption that schooling should assist with student viability: "it prepares our children to be good citizens and to lead good human lives" (1982, p. 20). It should prepare students to continue after graduation with further education or training, or, if they enter the workplace, to be able to learn on the job. Viable individuals are those who can change and grow with the world around them.

In the ideal, viability sounds good. In reality, how can it be implemented? I propose three goals, applicable for all students in K–12 schools as a way to implement the ideal of viability.

Goals of Universal Education

Universal education should strive toward integration rather than assimilation into American life. For much too long in U.S. history, schools have been used to assimilating students into a narrow conception of American life, as in the Anglo-conformity melting pot, which attempted to absorb selected students into a mold by replacing their native languages and cultures with the English language and "American ways," whatever that meant.

Many of these same schools operated on the specious assumption that certain students were not capable of entering the professions, thereby justifying their isolation and segregation of students by class, race, sex, and a host of other differences. Now is the time to reorient the emphasis of schooling toward integration into society—to strive to incorporate students into American life and global participation.

To *integrate* means to unite parts or elements to make a whole. With schools, integration works toward incorporation into a free society predicated on equality for all, and unity with diversity—e pluribus unum. Full integration into society is another matter and beyond the powers of the schools. Yet the schools can be inclusive, striving to facilitate the integration of individuals by providing requisite skills, knowledge, and attitudes.

Truly universal education must encompass all forms of diversity and be fully emancipatory, assisting students in the development of a disposition for lifelong learning. Universal education should foster the intellectual development of all students. I propose three goals for the intellectual development of all students:

1. Learning autonomy
2. Intellectual effectiveness
3. Cultural efficacy

If these goals are achieved, students will become lifelong learners able to carry on a meaningful life. Note that the goals are interrelated, but each takes a slightly different focus.

Learning Autonomy

In a free society, individuals must set their own goals and direct their own behavior. This is learned in schools when students are taught to be responsible for their behavior, including their own learning. This is the broadest of the three goals. Its focus is on behaviors within all domains of a student's schooling experiences, including social, personal, and cognitive learning. Addams, Du Bois, and Sanchez opposed education that predetermined students' futures often along very narrow, servile paths. They worked toward universal education that would allow students to determine their own futures by the goals they independently set for themselves and the vigor with which they worked toward those goals. Freedom requires that students become, in a sense, educational entrepreneurs.

Intellectual Effectiveness

Citizens need to be knowledgeable and wise. Schools can foster knowledge. In fact, schools are mandated by state accreditation standards to teach certain subjects. Universal education enables students to achieve intellectual competence in the subject matters taught in schools—knowledge that is important to students as individuals as well as to the greater society. Fundamentally, students should learn to think critically and creatively with the subject matter taught in schools.

Cultural Efficacy

Modern transportation and communications continue to shrink our world, as the cliché goes. But, as is often the case, the cliché is accurate. Today, more than at any time in history, each person must recognize that he or she is a member of a global society. This global society is multicultural and highly diverse. Cultural efficacy means that individuals recognize the diversity of humanity and are capable of functioning effectively in the global society, in addition to functioning within the closer confines of their home culture. This goal focuses on the students' ability to function as productive members of society, not merely in the narrow confines of a smaller cultural community.

Indeed, *home culture* may be variously defined for different purposes. In some cases, the home culture may be a specific local community, a generalized cultural community (the Latino community, the gay community), a religious community (the Mormon community), or a broader sense of home in the world, such as American, Canadian, or even North American or Western.

Universal education should engender a vision of the whole person—a global vision, if you will—and provide the intellectual means for individuals to participate meaningfully in that vision.

Conclusion

A disposition for lifelong learning can be nurtured if these three goals are achieved. Now that modern technologies have accelerated the pace of change, the once idealized goal of becoming a lifelong learner has become a practical necessity. Therefore, universal education should focus on the intellectual development of all students by fostering a love of learning—if not for the sake of learning as a philosophically worthy pursuit, then certainly as a mechanism for self-preservation.

The goals of universal education are not simply academic achievement standards, which can be subsumed in the goals. Rather, these goals aim at democratic ideals embedded in education for freedom in a diverse society. Critics and colleagues have commented, "Your goals boil down to just good education." I agree, adding there is nothing *just* in schools that do not foster viability.

Reflections

1. Explore how, in 1896, John Dewey implemented education for freedom in his University of Chicago Laboratory Schools. Describe how it started as a progressive system that ran from nursery school through twelfth grade.

2. Research Jane Addams and the Hull House, which was a progressive system that ran from nursery school to adult education.

3. Research the debates that occurred between W. E. B. Du Bois and another contemporary African American, Booker T. Washington, regarding industrial education. Analyze the rationale each used to support his position.

4. Analyze and describe the research results about early childhood intervention. For instance, what are the short- and long-term results of Head Start programs? Consider the following question: is compulsory, publicly funded preschool education a necessity to ensure equal educational opportunities for all children?

four

Honoring Culture and
Self-Identity

As students pass through classrooms each year, teachers have a limited amount of time to learn their names, discover who they are, and ideally, teach them something of value. Given the immense diversity of students and cultures, the task of truly understanding each and every student's culture is daunting, much less the unique characteristics of each student beyond culture. How, then, can teachers hope to identify and understand the diversity issues that arise in the teaching of students from many backgrounds? Moreover, having made these necessary discoveries, how can teachers help their diverse students understand similar issues as they make their way in the world?

To answer these questions I propose two essential attitudes for teachers. First, it is important for teachers to acknowledge—and work to understand—manifestations of human difference. Second, as part of such acknowledgment, teachers must know themselves well and come to terms with their attitudes toward human differences, recognizing their preferences, biases, and prejudices. To these ends, this chapter provides a nuanced explanation of human diversity in terms of culture and self-identity regarding issues such as race and ethnicity; sex, gender identity, and sexual orientation; English proficiency; and learning style preferences.

Family Culture

Culture is a means to survive and thrive learned through the shared experience of social interaction. Students are born into their respective culture and become competent individuals with unique self-identities to the extent they reconstruct the values, beliefs, attitudes, and behaviors learned from others within their culture. Social scientists call this phenomenon "the looking-glass self," a process of self-identity

51

formation through social interaction. Simply put, adults mirror to youngsters what is expected within the culture. The adults serve as role models of cultural expectations.

The family is a culture's most important institution. No culture can survive without it. In fact, a culture is really a community of families with shared experiences, values, beliefs, folkways, customs, and tools. Other institutions play a key role in any given culture, the school being paramount among them. Until the mid-1960s, in fact, schools were considered an extension of the family, and teachers in U.S. schools acted *in loco parentis*—in place of the parents—with parental rights, duties, and obligations for children similar to their parents. That doctrine has been replaced by a doctrine of individual rights: students and teachers have rights as individuals, such as right to expression, privacy, religion, and so on. This is a legal shift in viewpoints to ensure that students do not leave their constitutional rights at the schoolyard gate. Nevertheless, many still view schools as extensions of the family.

Family is not only culture's most important institution, but the individual's most important group. It fills many human needs. The list is long but includes love, intimacy, affirmation, protection, food, and health. Self-identity and resilience are first learned in the family. If students are lucky to be reared in a happy, nurturing, and loving family, they can overcome almost any obstacles life throws at them. If they are unlucky and are reared in an unhappy, dysfunctional family, they will more than likely face difficulties with life's challenges.

We should assume nothing about our students' home life, including the value of the structure of their families. There is no such thing as an ideal structure that works best for all families. Structures vary within and across cultures. In some cultures, families may be matrilineal, organized along the mother's biologic lines with the mother as head of household. In others, families may be organized along the father's lines. In others, grandparents, aunts, uncles, and other adult relatives play an important role.

Around the world, there has always existed diversity of family structures. What follows is a summary of current U.S. family structures. The *nuclear family* consists of a husband, wife, and children. The *extended family* consists of one or more nuclear families plus other relatives, such as grandparents, aunts, uncles, cousins, and so on. The *blended family* is made up of two previously married parents and the children of their former marriages. Among Native Americans, there is also a *tribal family* structure consisting of a clan of many families living in close proximity with the same functions as an extended family (Demo, Allen, & Fine, 2000).

Family structure means more than mere numbers. For example, the extended family entails much more than "more people." Among Mexican Americans, *La Familia* refers to children, parents, unwed mothers or fathers, grandparents, and possibly uncles and aunts who live in the same household or in close proximity. The elders are held in high regard and are involved in decision making. They may also serve as disciplinarians with the children, assist with some of the household chores, or help the children with homework, after-school functions, and so on. In their absence, aunts or uncles may serve their roles. The elders also serve as the holders of family traditions and stories, which they pass down to the children as they learned them from their own parents.

Among its many features, La Familia provides intergenerational bonding and cares for the elderly in a dignified environment. It solves many challenges faced by contemporary families, such as how to care for the elderly and how to assist children when the parent or parents work. I describe La Familia because of my personal familiarity. Other cultures adhere to their own traditional family structures and are worth learning about.

Family compositions have changed significantly. Many different kinds of single persons or couples serve as heads of households, such as gay and lesbian, interracial, and multiracial couples. For too long, people considered the ideal family composition to be the so-called nuclear family with a working father, stay-at-home mother, and the children. No doubt this ideal worked well for some, but the emphasis is misplaced. If the arrangement worked well, it was because the family was functional, loving, nurturing, and more or less happy. A good family life is the result of the quality of parenting and good luck, although structure and composition influence relationships within a family.

Few parents receive meaningful training for parenting. Yet good, "untrained" parents come in many variations, including gays and lesbians, multiracial individuals, single individuals both male and female, and heterosexual couples. In other words, students come to our classes from a variety of families, and we need to be sensitive about the variations.

Parental involvement in school activities poses a challenge for working parents. In a single-parent family, or a family where both parents work, time at home is precious and scarce. Parents have to plan evenings carefully to ensure they attend to their children's needs in and out of school. Helping with school assignments competes with other critical needs. Furthermore, because of younger children, a parent may not be able to leave the home to attend evening meetings or activities. Lastly, the parents may be too tired from work on the job and at home to expend much energy on school activities.

Some school activities and administrative and curricular materials may reflect a nuclear family bias. Some high schools still conduct a father-daughter banquet and dance each year, excluding all the girls who have no father, and of course all the boys. School records and forms sometimes ask children to fill in the names of their father and mother, rather than the names of their parents. In some communities, gay or lesbian parents may feel unwelcome at school functions, meetings, or activities. Or they may fear other children will tease their children, if word gets out their parents are gay or lesbian. Much of this can be ameliorated if the school and classroom are culturally responsive and welcoming of diversity, which is discussed in chapter 10 as building community in the school and classroom.

Students learn broad culture guidelines at home. Much of what parents teach is unconscious, starting with how they hold and talk to their infants. They live their values and beliefs and indirectly communicate them to their children through daily interactions. For example, as the father of twins, a boy and a girl, I found myself rough-housing my son more than with his twin sister. In this way, I realized later, I acted out the stereotypes that boys are strong and girls are fragile. My parents undoubtedly passed on these traditional gender stereotypes to me, and I conveyed them to my children. Traditional male-female role stereotypes (machismo versus delicacy, for example) are part of my Spanish-Mexican cultural heritage. Such machismo is also a stereotype attributed to Latinos, yet the same character traits that define Latino machismo are present in other cultures.

An individual's identity is influenced not only by family culture but also by race, ethnicity, sex, gender identity, sexual orientation, English language proficiency, and learning style preferences. Let's examine these more closely.

Race and Ethnicity

As social constructs, race and ethnicity are like two sides of a coin. While race and ethnicity differ, combined they are crucial to self-identity, language development, and socioeconomic status; they also influence gender identities and affect responses to sexual orientation issues. These terms are defined in many ways and are used interchangeably. They are often controversial when used for scientific, political, and other social purposes, especially the notion of race as a biological construct.

Race as a biological construct refers to the categorization of people into groups based on heritable characteristics. Visible traits include skin color, hair texture, and facial features. At best, race as a biological construction has rendered proof of physical diversity among people. At worst, the construct has rendered pseudoscientific findings to prove the ostensible intellectual superiority of the white race.

Race as a social construct has taken many different meanings, such as *culture, civilization,* and *ethnic group.* As a social image, race has many ramifications. In the 19th and 20th centuries, the term was also synonymous to *nation* and *tribe.* For example, historians wrote about the Greek race (civilization) and the Hebrew race (tribe). Similarly, I have heard people say that Martin Luther King Jr. was a credit to his race, meaning "ethnic group."

Ethnicity is a slippery concept. It refers to a person's identity with a certain group of people (*ethnos* is Greek for *people*). This identity includes an emotional and intellectual allegiance to that group—a sense of peoplehood and of identifying and belonging to some particular human group, as with the U.S. Constitution, which begins, "We, the people . . ."

Ethnicity as a social construct refers to categorization of people into groups based on ancestry, culture, religious, national, and even continental affiliations, such as European American or African American. Yet the terms often imply all European Americans are white and Christian and that Africans are all black, which is not the case. Nevertheless, race and ethnicity are often used interchangeably for self-identification and as social markers to define others.

Individual students may also use race, ethnicity, or a combination of both as self-identifiers and social markers. Or they may use other factors, such as gender, sexual orientation, or religion. Some view themselves as individuals without ethnic affiliation. Humans are too complex and too unique to be pegged into any one convenient label for self-identification, as we learn from the children of multiracial, multi-ethnic families.

Sex, Gender Identity, and Sexual Orientation

Like race and ethnicity, sex and gender are also like two sides of a coin. While they differ, combined they are crucial to self-identity.

For discussion purposes, I separate sex and gender identities. An individual's sex is biologically determined as male or female, although a small number of people are born with genitals for both. Gender, on the other side of the coin, is a culturally created social construct. What it means to be a man or a woman is defined from within the context of a given culture and is usually linked to a person's sex.

Gender definitions are linked to the biological features of a person's sex and may have arisen from the division of labor in the family. In most societies of the past, women worked in the home, bearing and caring for the children, cooking and cleaning the dwelling. Men worked outside the home, providing for and protecting their families. For much of human history, women were seen as subservient to men, a legacy still very much alive. But the rules of gender identity are in flux. Not long ago this struck me head-on when I walked into an airport men's room to find a young father changing his infant's diaper. His wife was outside on her cell phone texting her office. But what seems like merely role reversal in this situation is more significant renegotiation of gender identity. Such renegotiation happens in the macrocosm of Western society just as it happens in the microcosm of individual families, where two working adults must negotiate (and juggle) the once tradition-bound roles of homemaker and breadwinner. (For another perspective on ethnic and gender identity, see Sheets, *Diversity Pedagogy*, 2005.)

In school, girls who adopt a male gender identity and boys who adopt a female gender identity become frequent targets of ridicule or abuse. In the past, many teachers responded to "tomboys" and "sissies" by exhorting them to "act like a girl" or "act like a boy"—in other words, urging the students to adopt stereotypic gender roles. A contemporary approach focuses on teaching all students the broader value of diversity, which asserts every individual's right to behave as an individual, without regard for role stereotypes.

Modern researchers may argue the extent to which gender identity is influenced by the individual's sex (biology) or environment (culture). The conclusion most scientists make is that both forces are involved. The same is true for sexual orientation. Furthermore, my observation is that both gender identity and sexual orientation become apparent at various ages. The most that can be said is that sexual identity emerges within a child's first three years; gender identity forms more slowly, flowering sometime in elementary school, while sexual orientation becomes more certain later, usually during middle school or high school, sometimes in adulthood.

Sexual orientation is not a synonym for *homosexuality*. It has to do with an individual's sexual interest in members of the same or opposite sex, or both sexes, for fulfillment of love. My belief is that sexual orientation exists on a continuum from heterosexuality to homosexuality. An individual's sexual orientation manifests about the time of puberty or thereafter, when sexual interest awakens.

Same-sex orientation (homosexuality) is often confused with gender identity because of stereotypical representations. Gay males can be seen as having a female gender identity if they exhibit effeminate behaviors; lesbians can be seen as having a male gender identity if they exhibit masculine behaviors. In fact, gender identity and sexual orientation are quite different concepts, and many gay males and lesbians do not exhibit alternative gender identities. Except for matters of sexual affinity, they are indistinguishable from heterosexual males and females; gays and lesbians are not necessarily distinguishable by their mannerisms, speech patterns, modes of dress, or any other outward appearances.

While social prejudice against homosexuality is deeply embedded in Western history, cultural norms have varied from century to century and region to region; it is regarded as more "normal" in some areas of the world, more "perverse" in others. Although the pendulum is swinging toward greater tolerance and acceptance of homosexuality today, prejudice against homosexuals persists, especially in regions and communities dominated by conservative religious groups.

In 1973, the American Psychiatric Association reclassified homosexuality, removing it from the category of mental disorders and stating that it was, instead, simply a lifestyle. In other words, by psychiatric standards, gay and lesbian youth are not abnormal or mentally ill, though the experience of coming out may cause serious emotional trauma for the homosexual youth. Many may suffer from the alienation, fear of abuse, and downright abuse by others in school. The middle and high school years are crucial to self-identification, and the students may pass through turbulent periods of social isolation and alienation manifesting in anxiety, depression, demoralization, self-hate, and worse—suicide.

Indeed, students (usually in middle school or high school, more often the latter) who self-identify as gay or lesbian are likely to face many problems that arise from prejudice against homosexuals. Homophobia can also result in abuse directed toward heterosexual young people who behave in ways that are stereotypically gay or lesbian. Homophobic harassment is frequently directed at the children of homosexuals, even though the children themselves may be heterosexual (Baker, 2002).

Demographers may argue about the size of the homosexual population. Variations are based on how *homosexual* is defined. The Kinsey figure—homosexuals are 10 percent of the population—is still used most often as a rule of thumb (Kinsey, 1953), although this percentage may become larger as acceptance for homosexual youth increases and more come out.

Adolescents who identify as homosexual, even if only to themselves, adopt a highly stigmatized role. Ever since the study conducted by the U.S. Department of Health and Human Services titled *Gay Male and Lesbian Youth Suicide* (Gibson, 1989) was released, awareness has increased about the enormous number of students across the United States and Canada who are demonstrably at higher risk than heterosexual students for substance abuse and suicide. About 30 percent of homosexual youth have attempted suicide, and homosexual youth are three times as likely to kill themselves as are heterosexual youth.

Schools and classrooms can be lonely and often violent places for homosexual teens, with a high incidence of physical attacks against gay and lesbian students. However, after such attacks, it is often the homosexual youngster who is referred for disciplinary action—even though he or she did nothing to provoke an attack.

The fact is that schools are constitutionally obligated to provide a safe learning environment for all students, including gays and lesbians. In the 1990s, an openly gay student, Jamie Nabozny, sued the principals of his former middle and high schools in Ashland, Wisconsin, for not providing him protection from harassment and abuse (*Nabozny v. Podlesney*, 1996). The harassment started in seventh grade and devolved into violence that continued into high school. When a group of students pretended to rape him in full view of a larger group of students, the principal placed the blame on Jamie, telling him and his parents that harassment and abuse were to be expected and that he brought on the abuse by being openly gay. This was a classic case of blaming the victim. The principal did nothing to punish the abusers or provide protection for Jamie.

After the rape scene, Jamie fell into depression; his grades fell, he attempted suicide, and he dropped out of school. His parents sought competent counseling and medical assistance for Jamie, who was diagnosed with post-traumatic stress disorder. The circuit court ruled in Jamie's favor, and the U.S. Supreme Court allowed the ruling to stand. Jamie was provided monetary damages, and schools were informed they must provide a safe learning environment free from harassment and physical abuse as stipulated under numerous laws, such as in the Equal Access Act, Title IX, and the Equal Protection Clause of the Fourteenth Amendment of the U.S. Constitution. The court noted that Jamie's was not an isolated case. Many others had been brought to the courts, and today cases are still being prosecuted.

In some places, homophobia is so deeply ingrained in both community and school cultures that teachers and counselors often report fear of being ridiculed or harassed if they are seen to be supportive of homosexual teens. Some schools, either informally or by policy, discourage teacher support of gay youth or discussion of gay topics. I knew a homophobic teacher who badgered a youth he perceived as homosexual. The teacher verbally harassed the youth in classrooms and in extracurricular sports activities. When I spoke with the principal about the teacher's homophobic behavior, the principal defended the teacher, saying, "He uses the harassment as a motivational tool and doesn't mean anything by it." Whatever the teacher *intended*, it *resulted* in harassment. I should have confronted the teacher. Instead, I helped the youth transfer to another school where the climate toward homosexual students was a bit better.

Blatant homophobia also prevents many gay teachers and counselors from revealing their sexual orientation. Under these circumstances, highly professional, highly respected educators who might otherwise serve as positive role models for young people struggling with sexual orientation issues are prevented from doing so for fear of job loss through legal or extralegal means.

English Language Proficiency

Another aspect of cultural and self-identity is language. Many students enter school speaking English as a second language or speaking no English at all. But they may speak one or more other languages. These students are described as "English as a second language" students (ESL) or "English learners" (EL). I prefer the latter, because the students may speak two or more languages; English may be the third or fourth language, not the second.

The federal government uses the term *limited English proficiency* (LEP) to identify which students are eligible for programs such as bilingual education or ESL instruction. LEP refers to students who speak a language other than English at home and don't speak English very well, as reported by their parents. Under federal and state laws, school districts must have an objective means of determining the student's level of English proficiency.

Numbers and percentages of ELs are collected from various sources, mainly the 2000 Census and more recent surveys of the fifty State Departments of Education. The 2010 counts will undoubtedly show an increase. According to U.S. Department of Education reports (National Clearinghouse for English Language Acquisition, n.d.), exact figures vary, but at least one in five students, or 20 percent of students in preK–12 schools, are English learners. They are dispersed across grades: 10 percent of children in kindergarten, 7 percent in grades 1–5, and 10 percent in grades 6–12.

Spanish dominates other non-English languages because of the large number of immigrants from Mexico, the Dominican Republic, Cuba, and Central and South America. Vietnamese and Chinese follow. Still, there is much diversity among the languages spoken in schools today, such as the various national dialects of Spanish and Chinese. In addition, many other languages are spoken, reflecting Native American communities and many other countries (National Clearinghouse for English Language Acquisition, n.d.).

ELs are heavily concentrated in six states with the highest number of immigrants: California, Texas, New York, Florida, Illinois, and New Jersey. Yet immigrants and their children are dispersed throughout the United States, with the fastest growth of ELs in schools occurring in the Southeast, Midwest, and interior West. Immigrants follow resources and families. They move to places that provide economic opportunities and communities conducive for their families, including both rural and urban settings. (For a study of the status of ELs, see Orozco-Suárez, Orozco-Suárez, & Todorova, 2008. See chapter 6 as well for further description.)

Learning to talk is as natural as learning to walk. Humans have a built-in capacity for learning, processing, and creating language. All children acquire language as a part of natural maturation. They go through phases of listening, babbling, telegraphic speech ("Me hungry"), and irregular syntax patterns; my favorite phrase from childhood—"Daddy threw Mama from the train a kiss."

Children are equally capable of learning more than one language. In the United States and, to a lesser extent, in Canada, there has existed a belief that native bilingualism is abnormal. In Phi Delta Kappa's *Dictionary of Education*, the term *bilingualism* was described as detrimental to language development (Good, 1945). Currently, the study of bilingualism is much more objective. *Native bilingualism* refers to learning two languages concurrently during infancy and childhood years. My research found that some uninformed scholars believed native bilingualism impeded academic achievement in school subjects. This belief was based on a mistaken notion that children become confused when speaking more than one language, as do some adults when learning a second language. Second language learning for adults differs from early childhood language learning. The fields of language translating and language interpreting are reporting remarkable incidents of cross-cultural language translations and interpretations by children and adults, implying that the language capacity of humans appears to be much greater than previously assumed (McKee & Davis, 2010).

By the age of five or six, most children speak their native language with conventional syntax, using all of the sounds of that language. They know how to use the basic phonetic, syntactic, and grammar rules of the language. What they have yet to learn are all of the idiosyncrasies of the language, its nuances and idiomatic expressions.

Language is only one building block of what is called "communicative competence," which includes gesture, visual and vocal expressions, and such language-driven elements as speech, reading, and writing. Communicative competence, which begins naturally at birth, is aided by language instruction at school. Such language instruction must encompass the full range of communicative competence, including nonverbal communication. This is particularly true for students learning a second language—and thus a second cultural context.

Communicative competence is not necessarily bound by culture; some communication is universal, or nearly so, but it does develop and take place within a cultural context, often called nonverbal communication. Some elements, however, may be bound by culture. For example, simple gestures, such as the hand-waggling gesture that denotes "come here" among American youngsters, are not universal. In fact, the palm-up "come here" gesture typically seen in the United States and Canada is reversed as a palm-down gesture in certain Asian cultures.

Much of any message (meaning) exchanged in face-to-face communication is accomplished through gestures, facial expressions, and vocal intonations. In fact, words may be entirely absent. A mother's smile can be sufficient encouragement for a child to persevere in a difficult task; a mother's frown can discourage misbehavior.

Formal language learning in school, therefore, must include more than reading and writing if the aim is to help students who are learning a second language become more than merely literate but rather to become communicatively competent and thus able to convey meaning through nonliterate forms. At the same time, such formal language learning also must enable students to achieve academic competence, which is the ability to use language for higher-order thinking—to make and understand abstractions and metaphors, for example—without resorting to social cues. Communicative competence is socially functional language (in the roundest sense of the word *language*). Academic competence is required for the construction of meaning from texts and for interacting with ideas.

When working with second-language learners, it is important to distinguish communicative competence from academic competence. For example, students may be highly capable when using English at the communicative level without being very capable of using English at the academic level. One difficulty that arises in integrating new learners of English into English-only academic classes is that they often give evidence of communicative competence, and teachers mistakenly assume that communicative competence to mean that the students will be able to function successfully in the academic setting.

Bilingual education has emerged as a distinct field of study in teacher education. In the 1960s, it was a remedial program for Cuban immigrants and quickly expanded to serve Mexican American and other linguistic minority students. Throughout the 1980s and 90s, developmental programs were designed for monolingual, English-speaking pupils. Dubbed *immersion programs*, they embed pupils fully into a second language during the early grades, and by the middle grades, the pupils are fully bilingual. I know of such programs in Spanish, French, German, and Chinese.

Learning Style Preferences

How humans think and learn is one of the most robust areas of inquiry in our time. Early in the 20th century, scholars debated the issue of human intelligence as general aptitude versus intelligence as a composite of many singular aptitudes. Intelligence then—and only slightly less so now, at least in the popular mind—was tied to knowledge of the dominant culture. Thus it was argued that African Americans, Latinos, and Native Americans, for example, were less intelligent because they were less knowledgeable in terms of the dominant culture and because their race was genetically inferior.

Even today there are unresolved issues in the testing industry with regard to ensuring that standardized tests are culturally fair. I wonder if it is possible to construct a single test that is truly culturally fair. But that is only one problem regarding general aptitude intelligence testing.

Current thinking is that human intelligence is dynamic rather than static, consisting of multiple capabilities rather than just logical and linguistic. The capabilities manifest as the ability to create products, to learn from experience, and to solve problems. Harvard psychologist Howard Gardner developed a multiple intelligences theory along these lines. Originally, he posited seven manifestations of intelligence: logical-mathematical, linguistic, musical, spatial, bodily-kinesthetic, interpersonal, and intrapersonal (Gardner & Hatch, 1989). Later, he added a naturalist intelligence, or natural science, and an existential intelligence.

The theory has met varied responses. I have observed some crit-ics think Gardner's differentiation of the concept of intelligence is not grounded in science. Others argue that Gardner has identified propensities, aptitudes, or abilities, dubbing the theory as rhetoric or supposition. Many educators that I have observed appear to sup-port the multiple intelligences theory for its practical utility. Its use in schools and classrooms varies. Some teachers use it to try differ-ent approaches to teach certain material, especially when a particu-lar student is struggling with the way the material is normally taught. Some teachers provide activities to encourage students to utilize all the different intelligences. Some schools adopt multiple intelligence as a framework to guide teachers in their selection of instructional approaches.

Whether Gardner's theory is based on science or supposition is beyond the scope of this book. The theory has proved useful to teachers because it provides various means to teach any given topic. It has also provided a basis for speaking of the diversity of learning and teach-ing styles. Furthermore, the debate about intelligence has expanded. Intelligence is no longer thought of as static. Rather, a student's intel-ligences—plural—are dynamic and related to time, place, subject matter, and other factors. Viewing intelligence as dynamic rather than static means that teachers can identify specific student strengths and then use those strengths to extend learning in areas in which the stu-dent is having difficulty.

Acting on the theory of multiple intelligences, teachers also reify con-structivist learning theory, which posits that individuals construct knowledge by integrating new information into existing understand-ings. (See chapter 7 for discussion about constructivism.) Such con-struction takes place in the dynamic contexts of various forms of intelligence, or intelligences, to use Gardner's term.

Learning styles theory, which suggests that individuals learn in many different ways, complements multiple intelligences and constructivist theories. Truly effective teaching and learning must take all of these dif-ferences into consideration. Some students learn best by quietly read-ing, others by actively doing. In the search for an instructional panacea in the 1980s, much attention was paid to learning styles theory as a way of identifying how students learn best. The idea was that having identified a student's favored learning styles, the teacher then could tailor instruction so that the student could learn most effectively.

Unfortunately, the use of elaborate learning style inventories became, in some schools and school districts, another way to label groups of students. Individual differences were disregarded. Not surprisingly, this strategy failed, because of individual differences not accounted for in the learning style inventories. The point of attempting to determine how students learn best is to match teaching to individual learning styles. However, this misuse did raise a pertinent question: What about culture? Could at least some learning style preferences be culturally related? Perhaps so.

When I taught about demonstration speeches in my high school English classes in Wisconsin, I usually spent only a little time describing how to give a demonstration speech. (In this kind of presentation, the speaker shows how to do something.) I would give a brief example, such as demonstrating how to hold a golf club and swing it. Then I would ask for volunteers to give an impromptu demonstration speech. After a moment or two of initial shyness, invariably several volunteers would step forward and attempt to demonstrate any number of things. Boys volunteered to teach some sports move, like dribbling a basketball, kicking a football, and so on. Girls did not volunteer to demonstrate anything.

The lesson turned out differently when I tried it with Native American students going to school on the Crow Reservation in Montana. I thought I had established a good rapport with the Crow students. When I asked for volunteers to give the impromptu demonstration speech, I was disappointed that no one volunteered. At first, I took this to indicate I had done something wrong. I was puzzled. We turned to other subjects. Then, about a week later, five of the ten students in the class volunteered to give a demonstration speech—and they all did very well. Again boys volunteered. They demonstrated how to hold and play a Pow Wow drum and, just like the boys in Wisconsin, how to swing a baseball bat and dribble a basketball.

What had happened? Boys demonstrated, girls did not, and the boys took a week to prepare. I asked. The girls responded: "You're a man, and you demonstrated a man's activity—sports." Besides, none of their fathers played golf. They were curious about golf, having never seen a golf course. The boys agreed, except they had seen their fathers play sports. This occurred at a time when Title IX was barely emerging, and girls did not play sports. As I reflected on this incident, it occurred to me the Crow students were following the traditional pattern of learning and communicating that reflected their culture.

Often in classrooms, teachers communicate it is okay to take risks, to attempt a task or answer a question, even if a student is not sure about the answer. That is what I had done. I asked the Crow students to risk looking silly in an impromptu demonstration speech, on the assumption that it was a low-risk activity when undertaken before a teacher who gives every appearance of being trustworthy. On the other hand, traditional Crow culture takes a different tack. It emphasizes observation and study of a task first; then one practices the task for mastery before delivering a public performance, such as a demonstration speech in class. My Crow students were learning and communicating from the basis of a cultural tradition with which I was unfamiliar. In addition, most could not relate to my example because they had never seen a golf club or course. The girls thought sports were only for boys and assumed a demonstration speech was a boy's sport.

Supporting Student Identity

Schooling affects the development of self-identity. Teachers, administrators, counselors, and others in the school setting convey cultural attitudes without conscious intent. How teachers interact with one another in the presence of students, how they interact with students, and how they encourage students to interact with one another are forms of socialization by which culture is negotiated. (See chapter 10 for a discussion on building a culturally responsive classroom community.) On the institutional level, students are affected by the school's attitude toward their family culture and structure; their race, ethnicity, sex, gender identity, and sexual orientation; the availability and quality of support for English learners; and more. Schools constantly communicate what is valued, and what is not. The contents of the curriculum itself serve as a mirror of what is important to know. If students rarely see or experience curricular contents from their backgrounds, they may infer that their background is not to be valued as something worth knowing. (See chapter 9 for culturally responsive curriculum.) On the classroom level, students' self-identities are affected through unconscious social interactions with teachers. Students quickly sense a classroom that's inviting or uninviting, one that affirms or rejects. (See Sheets, *Diversity Pedagogy*, 2005, for promising practices with classroom interactions and identity.)

Teaching for diversity provides hope. Teachers need not act alone but should seek out like-minded teachers, students, parents, and others in the neighborhood to form a human social safety net. As adults, they can serve as role models for how to acknowledge and honor difference and make a difference with all youth. Good teachers acknowledge each student's unique identity while affirming that the student is part of a bigger community whose motto is e pluribus unum.

Reflections

1. Research the traditional family pattern of a recent immigrant family, or visit an Indian reservation and interview elders about the traditional family pattern of their tribe.

2. Self-identity based on race, sex, and sexual orientation is a growing field of study, especially with the growing numbers of multiracial families and adoptions by gay couples. Research and report on the various developmental models of identity that are emerging regarding race, sex, and sexual orientation.

3. Examine your intelligences using Gardner's notion of multiple intelligences. Also examine various scales that measure or identify personal traits or learning preferences. How do these measurements or scales accurately reveal who you are as an educator and as a human? Consider the limitations of measuring human ability or traits. Why do we even bother to measure or identify our traits in such a mechanical way?

Stand and Deliver

We live in dynamic times. Teachers must be intellectually dynamic, and they must help students realize a similar dynamism. You are challenged to stand and deliver, an exercise in critical thinking. Reflect on, discuss, weigh, and consider the event. Then, using the key concepts of the chapter, address the questions posed after the scenario.

New Kid on the Block

The Williams family moved from Atlanta to a sawmill town in British Columbia so that Mr. Williams could assist in automating the local timber mill. They were the first family from the southern United States ever to live there. They had one son, Leroy, whose African American parents died in a car accident when he was one year old. The Williams, a white couple, adopted him.

Leroy was in the seventh grade and attended the local combined middle-high school. Although he was gregarious and a good athlete, some students complained that he was "pushy" and "liked to argue a lot." One day during a volleyball game, Leroy executed an agile spike. Russ Schmidt, one of his team members, hollered, "Cool, boy!" (Lumbermen and others in the small British Columbia town commonly used the term *boy* to mean a person who is adept at getting what he wants.)

Russ tried to high-five Leroy. Instead of high-fiving, Leroy punched Russ in the nose, causing it to bleed. The teacher sent Leroy to the principal, who sent Leroy home with a letter for the Williams:

> Leroy is his own worst enemy. His classmates have bent over backwards to be nice to him, but he returns their friendship by arguing about almost everything. Leroy has been suspended from school because he provoked a fight during a volleyball game. Before he will be readmitted to school, he must apologize to Russ Schmidt, his classmate, for hitting him hard enough to cause a nosebleed and a black eye.

Leroy admitted to his parents that he had struck Russ Schmidt. He complained, "I wish we were back in Atlanta, where I was just one of the guys. Everyone here makes a big deal about my being black. Sure, they're just joking when they ask, 'Will your chocolate skin melt in the summer?' One girl asked how she could have a 'kinky' hairdo like mine. So when Russ kept calling me 'cool boy,' I got mad. They were all calling me 'boy.' I couldn't take it. It was more than the word, know what I mean?"

Questions

1. How are race, ethnicity, and identity involved in this incident? What about ethnocentrism and prejudice?

2. Were Leroy's new classmates being mean with their questions? Should they have known how he would react to the term *boy*?

3. Did the principal handle the incident properly? Why or why not? Think proactively. What should a school (principal and teachers) do to prevent such an incident?

five

Reducing Prejudice

I n culture, as in biology, diversity is essential for survival. Diversity is also ambiguous: cultural values, beliefs, and attitudes are ever changing, conserving, and adapting. Often, the only certainty is uncertainty. Culture ameliorates the tension between uncertainty and stability. In every culture, members must decide what to change and what to conserve. Rapid changes can be destabilizing, as in political revolutions that sometimes have undesirable ramifications. Excessive resistance to change can be oppressive and stifling to growth, as we see in countries ruled by dictatorships. Consequently, the price of healthy cultural survival is eternal vigilance to protect the balance between change and conservation. When this balance is upset—when a group feels its stability is threatened by contact with difference—the result can be prejudice.

This chapter opens with an examination of how culture influences perceptions of difference and the difficulty in describing difference without stereotyping. Next, it explores the origins of prejudice, prejudice reduction theories, and how educators can take a balanced approach to acknowledging and teaching about difference.

Cultural Lenses on Difference

Difference is not only inevitable, it is vital. Biological diversity is credited for the survival of all animal and vegetable species on earth. Consider turtles: there are many different species. Turtles are cold-blooded reptiles, some of which live in water (terrapin) and some on land (tortoise), but they are all turtles nonetheless, having survived for at least 200 million years. They have survived precisely because they are different and have adapted to cope with the exigencies of their varying environments. Human diversity functions similarly. People on every continent are fundamentally alike. We all need love, health, safety, food, and shelter, but we appear in many shades, shapes, sizes, abilities, languages, and cultures, adapting to survive.

Each culture sees and responds to this diversity differently. Within the context of culture, judgments vary on what is good or bad, right or wrong, or at times, simply neutral. This is the nature of culture. It teaches us values, beliefs, and norms of behavior. We develop a cluster of perceptions that shape how we define what we see, feel, touch, and otherwise sense and think. Simply put, we view the world—and all of our experiences—through the window of our culture, which serves as a screen to filter interpretations. Awareness of this universal phenomenon does much to open our minds to the possibilities of other ways of viewing and interpreting unfamiliar experiences.

In the teacher's lounge in Fairview Elementary School during recess, two fourth-grade teachers are talking about the new student in their pod.

Geri: Don't get me wrong. I like Mujahid. He's very polite.

Nicole: Always does his work?

Geri: You bet. And it's very neat.

Nicole: Sounds good to me.

Geri: That's just it. It's *too* neat. *Too* correct. Never a mistake.

Nicole: Not even a smudge. Yep, that's Mujahid, a perfectionist.

Geri: That's not normal—not for a fourth-grade boy.

Nicole: For a boy! Some of the girls are just as messy. What are you getting at?

Geri: Well, I'm not sure . . . that is, I'm not sure he's doing his own homework.

Nicole: Funny. Who would do it for him?

Geri: I'm not sure, but, well . . . okay, I'll say it, but it won't sound right. I think he's sneaky.

Nicole: Sneaky? Like in he doesn't do his own homework? What makes you say that?

Geri: Haven't you noticed? He sits in the back of the room. When I call on him, he drops his eyes. One time, I called him to my desk. He walked up very slow, looking at his shoes all the time. When I tried to talk to him, he just shuffled his feet and answered only yes or no. He didn't really try to talk with me.

Nicole: Of course, silly. He's very respectful. That's what I like about him. He's so polite. His dimples show when he smiles.

Notice the two teachers are talking about the same student. Geri sees a sneaky, distrustful boy who pretends to be sweet. Nicole sees a respectful, trustworthy boy who really is sweet. In their separate eyes, Mujahid is really two boys, each the opposite of the other. For Geri, the indirect eye contact and silent demeanor imply a sneaky student. For Nicole, the same traits imply a respectful student.

Luckily, the principal overheard the two teachers and explained. Mujahid was from Somalia, where he had attended an Arabic school that was very strict about deference to authority. At home and school, Mujahid was to defer to elders, parents, teachers, and other adults. Direct eye contact was considered rude, and youngsters weren't supposed to be talkative with adults. Also, the appearance and correctness of Mujahid's homework were a reflection on the family. So his father worked with him to get the work correct and neat, even if Mujahid had to redo the assignment many times.

Let's not be hard on Geri. Some students of all groups and sexes are sneaky, and they get somebody else to do their homework. She may have had other students who were sneaky. Therefore, she was speaking from prior experience. The point for us is to understand that, like Nicole and Geri, we too perceive individual differences through cultural filters. We view others according to how well they match or do not match images evoked from within our respective culture.

Consider a continuum of how we perceive individual differences. At one end, we may see differences as "variations on a theme." This stance views others as different without judgment. Others are human (the theme), and each is unique (variations on the theme of being human). It acknowledges a person is a unique individual, human and yet different. There is only one you, and one me—that's the way it should be. Each person displays individual characteristics that, taken together, form the whole fabric of human existence. No thread in this fabric is better or worse than another, though there may be different colors, textures, shapes, abilities, and so on. The phrase "It takes all kinds of people to make the world" captures this attitude.

At the opposite end of the continuum, we may see differences as "deviation from a norm." This stance is judgmental about human differences; it is not neutral. From this perspective, some individuals are seen as above or below the norm, as extraordinary, noble, eccentric, deficient, or weird. The judgment may be affirmative or negative, depending on its cultural context; the individual's differences may be admired, despised, or perhaps even tolerated but not fully accepted.

For example, a psychologist may label a person with developmental disabilities as *mentally retarded*. An older term for this condition was *feebleminded*. To the psychologist, the term is a scientific descriptor of an individual of a low mental age, as determined by credible examination. According to scientific language, this individual is not "normal"—that is, he or she does not have the mental age of average individuals, who set the level of the norm. Herein lies ambiguity, of course. To the psychologist, the evaluation is neither good nor bad. It is a fact that must be dealt with. But how do others perceive those terms and that difference? We often hear casual pejoratives such as "That's retarded!" applied to everyday situations that do not involve people with developmental disabilities, and yet disparage them indirectly.

Adults and children use labels to describe all kinds of differences, and the labels have consequences. At ten years old, I had to wear eyeglasses for nearsightedness. Unlike Harry Potter, I didn't look good in my rimless glasses. Other children called me "four eyes," implying I was weird or disfigured. My parents encouraged me to ignore the name-calling and told me to say: "Sticks and stones may break my bones, but words will never hurt me."

Not true. Words hurt. We still teach children that rhyme for self-defense against name-calling and labels, but for most of us, it doesn't work. Another expression is:

> I am rubber,
> You are glue,
> Everything you say

Bounces off me and
Sticks to you.

Again, we know those words aren't entirely true. Painful words stick to us, but who knows about the speaker? What other people think about us *is* important. Children quickly learn the painful power of words. It takes children much longer to understand that words are powerful only when they allow the words to hurt them. This is especially true of stereotypes based on ability, class, ethnicity, race, religion, sex, and sexual orientation.

Educators use labels as shorthand forms to communicate complex educational conditions. Yet it is all too easy to reduce those who are different from us to mere labels. "That student is African American" is sometimes used to say the student "acts African American," by which the labeler means the student behaves in ways stereotypic of African Americans. Or the label may not be stereotypic, but rather accurately identify the student's continental origin. Yet when you consider the diversity among African Americans, the label does not say much about the individual.

"That student is gay" can mean the student behaves in ways associated with homosexual stereotypes, such as flamboyant effeminacy—or the label may accurately identify the student's sexual orientation. Regardless, it says little about the individual, and such labels can ill serve those they characterize. The problem with many labels is not the label itself, but rather the connotations and stereotypes the label conjures. Much depends on how the label is used.

Labels can provide useful shorthand for discussion purposes. They can describe reasonable generalizations. For example, students who are labeled "ADD" have in common certain characteristics of attention deficit disorder. Students who are labeled "LEP" (limited English proficiency) have in common certain limitations in their understanding and use of English. But ADD students differ among themselves, just as LEP students differ from one another, often to a rather wide degree within the label's characteristics.

My point is simply this: teachers should examine what lies behind labels applied to students and recognize their limitations as well as their utility.

For example, critics of ADD contend the label is overused to describe any number of behaviors. Critics of the LEP label contend it stresses the negative rather than the positive attributes of non-English speaking students. (For a thorough discussion of labeling, see *Understanding Human Differences*, by Koppelman and Goodhart, 2005.)

We cannot ignore labels. Rather, we should understand how people apply labels to others and to themselves, and how to use them responsibly. Neither perspective—the variations on a theme or deviation from a norm—is always "right." Both views are interpretations. Take for example the biblical imperative "Thou shall not kill." In most cultures, a man who kills others as a serial killer is viewed as abhorrent and abnormal, while the soldier who kills others in defense of his country is judged a patriot or a hero who risks his life to save others. Another example is contemporary, and one I hear in not-so-civic discourse. Some say that a gay or lesbian person is simply different in sexual orientation; others see homosexuality as a perversion—a deviation from a norm. Differences are real, but how we interpret them is not fixed.

Let's examine how fixed interpretations of difference can develop into racism.

Origins of Prejudice

Like culture and self-identity, prejudice is learned through social interaction with others: at home, school, and in the broader community. It is a learned attitude about a group of people, learned from individuals who share something in common—for example, the same race, ethnicity, or sex—that the other group does not share. The attitude expresses itself in adverse opinions, dread, hatred, and fear of the other group. It manifests in discrimination against the group, as in institutionalized racism or sexism, or against an individual in the group. Such discriminatory actions at the individual level include stereotyping, name-calling, shunning, bullying, lynching, and at the social level, unfair practices, policies, and laws.

The genesis of prejudice arises from *ethnocentrism*, which is associated with ethnic group cohesiveness, as the term suggests. Individuals like their own cultures and its members. While ethnocentrism is often spoken of in negative terms, "good" ethnocentrism as well as "bad" exists. At its root, ethnocentrism means to focus or center on one's own culture, usually expressed in ethnic terms (hence *ethnos* for people) but now often broadened to include other factors such as gender, class, and race.

Ethnocentrism can range from exaggerated pride at one extreme to degradation at the other. Arrogant ethnocentrism is the attitude that one's group is superior to all others, that the group can do no wrong, as in the Nazi belief that "the Aryan race is superior to all others" during World War II. In the early 21st century, Osama bin Laden, leader of the terrorist organization al-Qaeda, waged war against those the group saw as "infidels" (all those who do not share the group's core beliefs).

Ethnocentric degradation, on the other hand, is the belief that one's group is inferior to others. Some individuals struggle against feelings of ethnocentric degradation when consistently bombarded by negative stereotypes about their group foisted on them in the broader community. African American psychologist Kenneth Clark drove home this point in his classic experiment, "White Doll, Black Doll" (Clark, 1955). In this experiment, he individually offered five-year-old African American girls a choice between two baby dolls of the same size and shape. The only difference between the two dolls was their color: one white and one black. The overwhelming choice was the white doll. When asked why they selected the white doll over the black doll, the girls said it was pretty, implying that the black doll was not.

In other words, the girls had learned to devalue their own skin color. They had not learned that black is beautiful. Furthermore, they had internalized the pervasive bias of the broader society in that era of blatant bigotry against African Americans (Clark, 1989). Children can be affected by degradation in the ways their ethnic group is portrayed in the media.

As a youngster, I was bothered from time to time with the negative stereotyping of Mexicans as lazy, cruel, or dishonest, such as in the U.S. portrayal of a Mexican Santa Claus as "Pancho Claus." He was a jolly, lazy man who got drunk on Christmas Eve and could not deliver Christmas presents. Needless to say, I did not like the "Mexican" Santa Claus. At least the white one delivered presents on time. As a boy,

I did not know that Santa Claus was not, according to my Mexican friends, an important Christmas character in Mexico or most of Latin America, much less a drunken, ugly stereotype.

I also recall the *Frito Bandito* television commercials of the 1960s that depicted a Mexican revolutionary as a short, fat, bearded man wearing a sombrero, ammunition belts crisscrossing his chest, and a pistol in each hand. With a thick "Mexican" accent, he stole Fritos from children as they played on neighborhood sidewalks and yards. The gutless thief who steals from children was enough to make me ashamed of my cultural background.

Purveyors of mass media have become more conscious of its effects and are much more careful about the images projected. In a broader sense, however, arrogant ethnocentrism and ethnocentric degradation still exist, often in more subtle tones or textures. Currently, pejorative images of Arabs and Islamics are pervasive.

Up to now, I have described the two extremes of the ethnocentrism continuum. In the middle is a range of good ethnocentrism. This middle ground, which I call "mild group pride," is seen almost daily. It is the normal feeling that one belongs to a pretty good group and is often associated with self-esteem. Mild group pride is apparent when a group gathers to observe a holiday—or creates a celebration—to foster group pride and public awareness, such as the annual gay pride days in June celebrated in cities across the United States.

Most of us have experienced mild group pride; some have experienced tinges at the extremes of arrogance and degradation. And most of us are guilty of some prejudice and discrimination in stereotyping of another group. It is important for us to remember that our prejudices are learned, and they can be changed. Most of us hold prejudices. The answer to "Am I prejudiced?" is "Yes, more or less. I am human." Don't fret.

Ignorance is the most common cause of prejudice. We simply don't know the objects of our prejudices—the people and their cultures—but once we come to know them by gaining new knowledge and insights, we are able to modify our prejudices, if not eliminate them entirely, by keeping our minds open to diversity.

Prejudice Reduction Theories

I have wrestled with teaching approaches to reduce prejudice. One approach I used in prejudice reduction workshops was through moral admonitions: directly address the prejudice so that individuals will understand why their attitude is morally wrong and then change it. In other words, persuade or cajole prejudiced individuals to change their attitudes. The approach had questionable efficacy. At best, it provoked guilt and temporarily raised the individual's awareness of the prejudice, but as the guilt waned, so did the resolve to change. At worst, the approach provoked denial. The individual felt attacked and resisted the charge of prejudice. He or she did not acknowledge the prejudice and did not feel a need to change, rationalizing he or she did not have "that problem." If no perceived problem existed, there was no need for a solution. I called this the "no-problem problem." I shared the no-problem problem with colleagues, and discovered they had abandoned it as bad teaching. Upon further reflection, I abandoned it, too.

In my search for prejudice reduction approaches, I discovered other, more efficacious approaches, which I call the contact thesis and the education thesis.

Contact Thesis

The contact thesis is based on the assumption that people are fair-minded and will change their attitude through direct experience with individuals of a different group. This approach was applied with the intergroup education method of the late 1940s and 50s, and again in the school desegregation attempts of the 1960s and 70s when white and black students were bussed to each other's schools. One idea behind intergroup education was to place students of different races together in the hope they would interact positively (Banks, 2005). However, once in the schools, the youngsters often resegregated into black and white groups. Both the intergroup and desegregation attempts placed emphasis on achieving intergroup contact but experienced difficulty sustaining the contact.

Mere contact is not enough. To sustain contact, I have tried using cooperative learning activities to reduce prejudice with my college-age students. I asked a mixed group of students to work together as equals on a common learning task over a sustained period of one semester. (For context, my campus is large with thirty thousand students, and most of my students are strangers to each other.) At the end of that time, the students had bonded, learned much, and their prejudices were reduced, according to their self-reported feedback. Feeling successful, I continued to conduct the same experiment for five years in the same course. Overall, the students reported improvement of both their understanding of the material, and of each other. Perhaps the students' improved knowledge and attitude occurred because they volunteered for the experiment? This is known in research parlance as the *Hawthorne effect* (Harvard Business School Library, 2009). The students felt good about the special project, which motivated them to improve. I continue the experiment, however, believing the sustained contact enables students to become familiar, which fosters positive attitudes toward each other. This, in itself, makes the experiment worthwhile. (See chapter 10 for more on cooperative learning, especially the Stand and Deliver exercise at chapter's end.)

Education Thesis

The education thesis is the second prejudice-reduction approach I developed. It is based on the assumption that people are fair-minded and will change their attitudes when presented with new information about a particular group. The education thesis is developmental and focuses on the acquisition of knowledge at three levels of literacy: (1) functional, (2) cultural, and (3) critical.

Functional Literacy

Functional literacy refers to the ability to speak, understand, read, and write one's native language or, in practical terms, the dominant language of the society in which one lives. For most of the United States and Canada that language is English, though French is the language of Quebec, and Spanish is nearly essential in parts of the U.S. Southwest. Functional literacy also refers to the basic information an outsider would need in order to cope adequately within another culture. In short, functional literacy is introductory.

Cultural Literacy

Cultural literacy stands on the base of functional literacy and refers to an increased knowledge about a particular group (Hirsch, 1987). While a certain amount of cultural literacy can be gained intuitively, that intuitive knowledge is refined through functional literacy—for example, by reading and listening to cultural information—and is further enhanced and enlarged through critical literacy, or thinking critically and creatively about shared cultural information (discussed later). This is the essence of a student's intellectual development—reading, reflecting, and acting on the knowledge gained from many different cultures.

The pertinent question in attaining cultural literacy is, "Which culture?" Three intellectual camps dominate the arguments over this question. Should cultural literacy be Eurocentric, Afrocentric, or multicultural? Each of these camps merits a short exploration.

Eurocentric cultural literacy is based on a belief that in Western civilization, the traditions and cultures of Europe should be regarded as cultural exemplars. Knowledge of greatest worth, according to Eurocentric tradition, is derived from the European cultures and their roots in ancient Greece and Rome. For the Eurocentrists, the best curriculum is one that draws from this European heritage (Adler & Wolff, 1959).

Afrocentric cultural literacy is based on a belief that Western culture, in fact, has strong roots in African cultures. Ancient Greece was indebted to Africa for much of its development. Furthermore, modern North American culture is much indebted to African influences by way of the slave trade, which brought not just strong hands and backs but also strong traditions of history, language, music, and art. Afrocentrism is not simply an African American reaction to the predominance of Eurocentrism. Rather, it is an ethnocentrism that adherents believe harkens to a deeper, more accurate cultural history of the Americas. For the Afrocentrists, the best curriculum is one that draws from African heritage (Harris, 1992).

Multiculturalism is, in a sense, a middle ground. This type of literacy posits that Western civilization cannot be linked solely with either the European cultural history or its supposedly deeper roots in African cultures. Rather, multiculturalism suggests that North American culture, as a whole, is a culture of pluralism and diversity—in fact, many cultures. These cultures retain distinct identities and are interdependent as their members work toward common values, beliefs, and goals in order to nourish a cohesive unity: "American" society or "Canadian" society. Students should be provided opportunities to read, weigh, and consider the world of ideas of many cultures, rather than be restricted too narrowly on any given culture (see chapter 9 for a discussion of teaching about cultures).

Moreover, the concept of culture under the rubric of multiculturalism is broader than ethnic, racial, linguistic, or national heritage. Culture also includes a variety of other factors by which humans form collectivities or communities, however loosely knit. Such factors include family, gender, sexual orientation, economic status (or class), ability or disability, and so on.

A multicultural view of cultural literacy, then, is that such knowledge should focus on the construction of meaning based on multiple perspectives: one's own culture, the culture of the society at hand, and the global culture as expressed through common concerns and values. Ralph Waldo Emerson, the American essayist, said that each generation must write its own books and find its own solutions to problems.

Critical Literacy

Finally, *critical literacy* refers to the ability to think critically and creatively and is the highest (most intellectually sophisticated) form of literacy. To be critically literate in the ethnic studies context means to be able to analyze, synthesize, and evaluate information of many types (literary, historical, scientific) and from various sources (reading, observation, research). Individuals who are critically literate are able to make inferences, draw conclusions, generalize, predict outcomes, and engage in other aspects of critical and creative thinking, as discussed in chapter 8.

Now that I've described the origins of prejudice and explained the philosophical bases behind various approaches to reducing it, let's examine how educators teach about and to cultural differences in a positive way.

Proactive Approaches to Culture in Education

Culture is multifaceted, and for purposes of discussion, some narrowing is essential. Thinking in terms of a student's cultural background is a useful framework for better understanding the individual student and, in many cases, groups of students from similar backgrounds.

However, educators must ensure that their interactions with students, their expectations for student learning, the curriculum, and any cultural awareness programs are free from hidden or explicit bias.

One opening imperative is that educators must disregard the idea of high and low cultures. There is no "norm" that cultures deviate from. Cultures are neither better nor worse than others; they are merely different from one another. An elitist notion of culture would hold, for example, that people who read Shakespeare and listen to classical music are high culture (therefore culturally superior), whereas people who read supermarket tabloids and listen to rockabilly music are low culture (therefore culturally inferior).

"White trash" and "trailer trash"—pejorative characterizations for impoverished whites—are stereotypic labels that are as much identified with so-called low culture as with low socioeconomic status. Students who are assigned low-status labels on the basis of cultural elitism often have a more difficult time in school because they not only must overcome such real limitations as poverty, but they also must overcome the stigma of assigned cultural inferiority. When a student so labeled has trouble learning, it is too easy to say, "Well, what would you expect from a kid from that kind of family?" And so the victim of stereotyping is further victimized. Educators must be vigilant that their interactions with students and learning expectations for students do not reveal bias toward an "elite" culture.

The challenge of cultural elitism also extends into the curriculum, for example, when teachers adopt a "heroes and holidays" method for teaching about other cultures, putting emphasis on the leading figures within a culture. Such a method provides only token recognition of diversity, often delivered in ways that are at best patronizing and at worst superficial. This method diminishes the dominant U.S. culture, for example, by reducing Revolutionary War–era history to Washington's birthday, now lumped with Lincoln's as President's Day. One hears about the heroes General George Washington and Colonel Ethan Allen without learning about the men and women who made the heroes. (For a Revolutionary War account from the perspective of one of Ethan Allen's foot soldiers, see Raymond J. Rodrigues's *Memoir of a Green Mountain Boy*, 2007.)

While such diminished representations are superficial, even the best cultural awareness programs in schools have limitations. It is extremely difficult to teach the deeper aspects of any culture, because a culture is like an iceberg—most of it lies below the surface submerged in the flow of family and community life. At that subconscious level, culture determines the behaviors and attitudes that are defined as good or bad, acceptable or unacceptable, worthy or unworthy. These values and beliefs manifest in and are reinforced by the rituals, folkways, traditions, and tools that are the visible part of the iceberg.

We can teach *about* a student's cultural background, and we can help those outside the culture participate in cultural rituals, but it is next to futile to attempt to teach people a culture at the subconscious level. This is an important understanding. One learns such things by *living* in the culture, and even then impressions are singular. Nonetheless, each student is a unique individual with the capacity to contribute to others and benefit from the contributions of others. Studying other cultures can increase self-awareness and awareness of others. At times, students learn about a culture indirectly, which is often referred to as the "hidden curriculum."

The school curriculum, however, is not hidden. It is intentional, although one may not consciously understand its underlying cultural values and beliefs. Studying famous men—Washington, Lincoln, Martin Luther King Jr.—may help define what the school culture considers to be good or important in the civic culture. Studying classic English literature—Shakespeare, Chaucer—can do the same. These examples might point to a high culture and a hidden curriculum that is elitist and male-oriented, or, depending on how famous men and classic literature are juxtaposed with other curricular choices, might simply be part of a balanced approach to culture.

A balanced approach sends many powerful messages. First, the student's culture is affirmed. Second, other cultures are affirmed. Thus students see that though differences exist, connections also exist. (Teachers have much to balance in their curricula. Chapter 9 provides detailed information on curriculum development.)

Reflections

1. Do a reality check on the state and school district in which you reside. You should find online data compiled by your State Department of Public Instruction of the state's school demographics. Find out how many immigrants (total number and percentage of population) reside in your state and how many ELs or LEP students attend school. Look further at the communities where the immigrants reside, and research what the community and schools do to assist the immigrants and their children. Do the same with the school district in which you reside.

2. Research the topic of degradation, as it currently manifests. I described it with Clark's experiment involving white and black dolls (Clark, 1955). The experiment has been replicated with similar results. How else might degradation manifest?

3. Like biological diversity, human diversity is an obvious fact of life. Yet sometimes what is obvious is not always apparent. Sometimes we can't, as the saying goes, see the forest for the trees. Following is a game to teach students about human diversity that makes sure the obvious is noticeable.

An Apple a Day Keeps Stereotypes Away

At the market, buy ten or fifteen of the same kind of apples, such as Red Delicious. Convene a group of others, and seat them in a circle. Place a small table or bench in the center of the circle. Stand in the circle, and ask their assistance with a tasty experiment. Give them each an apple. (They can eat it after the experiment, that's the tasty part. First, the experiment, however.) Ask them to become familiar with the apple and really get to know it by inspecting, touching, even smelling it. Ask them: What does it look like? What are its distinct markings? Nicks? Bruises? What about the color and hue? How does it smell? Then ask them to give their apple a name. This is essential. After they are done, collect the apples and place them on the table, jumbling them together into a pile.

Ask the group to stand and gather around the piled apples. Then say, "Look. They appear to be the same. Pick out your apple, and please return to your seats." After discussions among themselves, each will take his or her apple. When they've reconvened, ask them to tell the name of their apple and how they selected it from the pile of like apples.

What should happen is that each participant will identify the uniqueness of his or her apple, describing in some detail the uniqueness of the apple, even though it by-and-large looks the same as the others. The experiment reveals important facts—we are more alike than different, but differences matter—by making several points:

- Each apple (like humans) has similar characteristics to others in the group.

- Each apple has differences that make it distinguishable; like humans, each is unique.

Another important fact revealed by the experiment is that we have relationships with individuals, not groups:

- As with each apple, the better we know an individual, the better we can know his or her uniqueness.

- As with each apple, the better we know the individual, the less apt we are to stereotype members of his or her group.

What happens if a student can't find her apple? This does happen and provides an exciting teaching moment. Let's say a student, Gretchen, looks puzzled. She can't seem to figure out which is her apple. "They all look the same." She is correct. You notice that at first glance, they do look the same, and like people, it takes a while to get to know them. Same with Gretchen. She needs more time to examine the uniqueness of her apple. In other words, it takes a while to become acquainted with others well enough to distinguish them as individuals. The experiment is rich with possibilities for discussing human diversity. Feel free to expand on it for your teaching purposes.

six

Understanding the Achievement Gap

U
p to this point we have examined various cultural and educational factors to establish a basis for identifying and understanding diversity in the classroom. Lest we forget, students are more alike than they are different. In the main, we should think of them as individuals rather than members of a group. Yet group affiliations influence individuals, students, and teachers alike. At times, we should acknowledge group differences in order to provide all students an equal opportunity to learn. This chapter explores the impact of sociocultural factors such as poverty, race and ethnicity, English language proficiency, gender, and sexual orientation. While none of these factors will "fate" a student for high or low achievement, the achievement gap between various groups is real. Understanding the impact of these factors is the first step to ameliorating any difficulties students may experience. The chapter also discusses the policy of equal educational opportunity as a strategy for accommodating group and individual differences.

The Impact of Poverty

The figures are daunting; poverty is on the rise. Many of the personal challenges caused by poverty are beyond an educator's ability to improve, but educators do make a difference in the lives of their students. This is why good educators stay with teaching. They know education has long been a vehicle toward equality, and that what they are doing is serving to uplift their students and the greater community. These words are not merely the fluffy pie-in-the-sky mutterings of a dreamer. They are based on a lifetime of engagement in education where I have observed teachers assisting students to think and do for themselves—to become viable individuals.

Poverty has a rude way of butting its all-too-loud voice into this lofty discussion. "Get real," it says. "I'm not going away just because you wish I would!" Poverty can thwart the greatest of intentions. So let's be realistic but keep our ideals. Let's take a close, hard look at poverty, the academic gap that reflects the impact of poverty, and then what educators can do to ameliorate its impact on students. Let's also examine what parents can do to make a difference in the lives of their children.

Poverty is pervasive—ingrained in some neighborhoods, scattered in some, and invisible in others, but overall real and on the rise. According to the U.S. Census Bureau (2009), the official poverty line in the United States is about $18,400 annual income for a family of four. Also, 13.2 percent of the nation's population lived in poverty in 2008, consisting of approximately 39.8 million people, an increase from 37.3 million in 2007. Most demographic groups experienced an increase in poverty from 2007 to 2008. The poverty rate increased for:

- Whites, 8.6 percent in 2008, up from 8.2 percent in 2007
- Asians, 11.8 percent in 2008, up from 10.2 percent in 2007
- Latinos, 23.2 percent in 2008, up from 21.5 percent in 2007
- Children under eighteen years old, 19.0 percent in 2008, up from 18.0 percent in 2007

Poverty rates in 2008 were unchanged for African Americans at 24.7 percent and for Native Americans at 23.2 percent.

With *situational* poverty, there is a ray of hope. This poverty is circumstantial and potentially temporary, as when a family is bankrupted by medical bills due to a catastrophic illness. Over time, the family may emerge from bankruptcy with hard work and assistance from various support systems. *Generational* poverty is more permanent. It refers to a person or family who has lived in poverty for two or more generations. This kind of poverty is difficult to alleviate because of its ingrained history, making it almost intractable.

Students from low-income backgrounds are different than their middle-class peers, and in ways that go beyond money or test scores. Having less money does not mean they are less intelligent, and yet more adults treat them as though they are not as capable as their middle-income peers, by holding or expressing lower expectations. These adults may include, wittingly or not, the student's teachers, parents, and others in the community.

What others believe and translate into expectations for poor children is what poor children may come to believe. Individuals living in poverty, particularly generational poverty, may come to believe (not without justification) that they are not in control of their lives—indeed, that controlling their lives is beyond their power or ability. Impoverished persons often express fatalistic attitudes such as "Failure is inevitable when you're poor" and accompany such attitudes with despondency such as "Things will never get better." These individuals may have low expectations for themselves and for their children: "If failure is inevitable, why try?"

For educators, the key point is this: teachers who expect children to succeed create students who succeed. In the reverse, teachers who expect children to fail create students who fail; teachers who give up on the potential of their students catalyze a self-fulfilling prophecy. Students live down to their teachers' low expectations.

Most teachers are not consciously biased against low-income students, though some may unknowingly discriminate by behaving as though poor students are less capable or willing to learn. These teachers may even express sympathy with or pity for these youngsters. Yet in these teachers' minds, such factors as less money, dated apparel, and less elegant language equate to less capacity and drive than children who are more advantaged. Teachers are also affected by a student's lack of background knowledge, assuming if a student is not at grade level, or if the student doesn't get a lesson because of a different experiential background, he or she is a "lost cause" or "too late."

Based on my observations and reading, here are some indicators of lowered expectations at work. The teacher:

- Communicates with and calls on low-income students less often
- Makes eye contact less often and gives students less time to respond to questions

- ❑ Praises low-income students less frequently than middle-income students when they risk answering questions about which they are unsure
- ❑ Criticizes low-income students more often than middle-income students for giving inaccurate responses to questions
- ❑ Provides fewer details and less precise feedback to low-income students
- ❑ Demands less homework and effort from low-income students

These actions are only indicators of possible social class bias. Teachers should hold high expectations for all of their students and then work with the students to achieve success. This calls for sensitivity to the student's cultural background and current circumstances, but neither dire circumstances nor cultural background should be cause to lower the teacher's expectations. Remember, the current federal policy embedded in No Child Left Behind requires more than an attitude that all children *can* learn; it requires that all children *must* learn. Yet it is often easier for teachers to dumb down lessons or allow a student to slide rather than address teaching and learning challenges head on.

The challenges are real. Poverty and its social ramifications can affect the development of both communicative and academic competence, especially the latter. But there are solutions. Federally funded Head Start and similar programs provide early education on the premise that supplementing impoverished students' home language experiences will help the children succeed in academic learning along with their more advantaged peers. Assessments of the early childhood programs show a positive impact on the academic performance of low-income children in the primary grades (Zigler, 2010). There are classroom resources as well. For example, Tileston and Darling's *Why Culture Counts* (2008) provides research-based strategies for adapting instruction based on experiential backgrounds of diverse, low-income learners.

Individual teachers who seek solutions and refuse to accept defeatist beliefs make a positive difference in the lives of poor children, and in turn for their families. Educators can help families understand how critical high expectations are to success, how education can help children rise out of poverty, and what parents can do to support their children's education.

Much research has been conducted on parent-child relationships in poor families. In my experience, one factor consistently emerges—children will emulate their parents. For example, parents who read and who read to their children discover that their children will have less difficulty in school. If children see their parents reading and talking about what was read, they will desire to do the same. Likewise, when parents read and discuss stories with their children, they enhance the language development of their children. This simple act cannot be overemphasized. It does so much with so little. Books are available at public libraries if parents can't afford to buy them. For example, I encourage Latino parents, who are more comfortable speaking and reading in Spanish, to read with and to their children in Spanish. Reading and discussing the story or information in any language will enhance the child's language development in any language, including English.

In short, teachers have a choice between being what I call an "allocator" or an "equalizer." Teachers who buy into class bias are role allocators. They assign students certain life roles, not necessarily directly, but by the ways they teach the students. Often they channel students from middle-income families into the education conduits that lead to professional, high-status, high-pay careers, while channeling impoverished students into the education conduits that lead only to low-status, low-pay employment. This channeling can be embedded in the school's own systems. Some large and middle-size school districts in the United States and Canada rely heavily on ability grouping and tracking. Classes or groupings in the low track are intended for students with low ability and tend to be utilitarian, emphasizing rote memorization and completion of workbooks, while the middle and higher tracks emphasize higher levels of critical thinking such as drawing inferences and making judgments.

Supporters of academic tracking claim that placement is based solely on intellectual ability. However, in most tracking systems, there is a high correspondence between the students' social class and their placement in a given track, beginning as early as the fifth grade. Once placed in the low track, it is almost impossible to advance from it. This is not surprising, given what we know about the possible effects of poverty on academic development and lowered expectations. Teachers must be on guard when they work in schools that serve as sorting machines whose main purpose, though never stated as such, is to mirror and maintain social stratification.

Educators who help all children fulfill their potential to the best of their ability, regardless of socioeconomic status, are equalizers. These are the educators who are committed to the core beliefs of equality, e pluribus unum, and mutual respect. They work to achieve, to the best of *their* ability and for every student, the goals of universal education: autonomous learning, intellectual effectiveness, and cultural efficacy. This is indeed a grand design, one that can lift up those in poverty and fulfill Horace Mann's vision of the school as the great equalizer—a promise yet to be fully realized.

The Impact of Race and Ethnicity

In the last chapter I mentioned that race and ethnicity were slippery concepts that can be confusing. Despite the confusion, the terms *race* and *ethnicity* have useful purposes for teachers. Throughout this book, I have addressed human differences as assets rather than liabilities. There are times when differences are a liability, however, such as differences in high school completion rates and academic achievement.

For many obvious reasons, it is important for students to complete high school. High school diplomas lead to higher incomes and higher occupational status. Furthermore, high school dropouts are more likely to live in poverty, require public assistance longer, and be involved in crime more than high school graduates.

The National Center for Education Statistics (NCES, 2009), a branch of the U.S. Department of Education, defines a high school dropout as an individual sixteen to twenty-four years old who is not enrolled and has not completed high school. Boys drop out of school twice as much as girls. Asians have the lowest dropout rates of all groups, with about 97 percent of the Asian student population completing high school; the second highest group is white students at a 94 percent completion rate.

The percent of dropout rates has lowered over the past few decades, although there is a considerable difference among the dropout rates for whites, African Americans, and Latinos. See table 6.1 for the respective percentages.

Table 6.1: Dropout Percentages by Race/Ethnicity

Year	White	African American	Latino
1980	11.4	19.1	35.2
1990	9.0	13.2	32.4
2000	6.9	13.1	27.8
2007	5.3	8.4	21.4

Source: NCES, 2009

A higher percentage of whites complete high school compared to African Americans and Latinos. For whites and African Americans, the dropout rate has lowered considerably when the 1980 percentages are compared to 2007. For Latino students, the decrease in dropouts has not been as sharp for the same time period. High Latino dropout rates are partly the result of the high proportion of immigrant students who never attended high school in the United States.

In addition to the differences in dropout rates among whites, African Americans, and Latinos, there is a persistent academic achievement gap among the three groups. The National Assessment of Educational Progress (NAEP) reports on achievement in the core academic subjects: reading, writing, mathematics, science, and social studies. It has assessed student academic performance since the 1980s and provides a profile on the extent student performance has changed over time, including the achievement gap between whites, African Americans, and Latinos.

On NAEP assessments, whites consistently outperform African American and Latino students (NCES, 2009). For example, in 2007 at the eighth-grade level, African Americans scored twenty-seven points lower on reading assessments than whites, and Latinos scored twenty-five points lower than whites. This is not atypical. In many schools and districts, these results are replicated in local and state tests of academic achievement as indicated by students' grades in school. The gap persists in all the school subjects assessed by the NAEP, although the gap is slowly closing over the years since it has been measured.

The NAEP assessments, which are a rather recent development of the 1980s, reiterate a long-standing observation that most minority students do not perform as well on academic tasks as do white students. Before the existence of NAEP assessments, scholars, educators, and policy makers speculated on the gap, and at times, tempers rose with heated debates about the causes of the gap. Did it occur because minorities were inherently inferior to whites? Was it that poor performance mirrored the minorities' low socioeconomic status? Or were the schools biased against minorities and thereby failed to serve them as well as whites?

Among the debating parties there was little consensus, except that an achievement gap existed—but why? A simple question, but the answers are far from simple. For discussion, I have clustered the usual answers into four categories of interpretation: (1) cognitive deficit, (2) environmental deficit, (3) unequal access to knowledge, and (4) cultural incompatibility.

Cognitive Deficit

This interpretation is no longer considered valid, but teachers should be aware of it, because it still comes up occasionally. The cognitive deficit idea was based on the pseudoscience of eugenics of the late 19th and early 20th centuries. Eugenics was premised on the belief that white races were superior to non-whites. Hence, through selective breeding and sterilization of non-whites, inferior races could be bred out. Eugenics did much to lend support to the pervasive racism of the times, and its impact is still with us today. Through eugenics, early 20th century researchers and theorists argued that Latino and African American students were "hardwired" with less intellectual ability than whites. Because Latino and African American students possess less capability for intelligence, the cognitive-deficit proponents reasoned, it is futile to expect such students to achieve beyond that limited intellectual capacity; in other words, it is futile to expect them to perform as well as white students. For interested readers who seek an overview on eugenics in the United States, Wikipedia provides an accurate account of the movement (http://en.wikipedia.org/wiki/Eugenics). Also, for an excellent, though old book that's relevant to educators interested in the link between eugenics and the cognitive deficit, read Stephen Jay Gould's *The Mismeasure of Man* (1981).

If African American and Latino students are cognitively programmed for lower-level intellectual achievement, then academic intervention programs are of little use. Therefore, the cognitive-deficit proponents suggested it would be in the best interests of Latino and African American students for schools to prepare them for the trades, rather than the professions, for which they are intellectually better suited. For example, don't teach them to be landscape architects; instead, teach them to be yard workers. This line of reasoning is precisely what W. E. B. Du Bois and George Sanchez vigorously opposed. Vocational tracking and ability grouping tread dangerously close to the trap of cognitive deficit.

Environmental Deficit

The second interpretation for the cause of the achievement gap argues that most Latino and African American students are not themselves cognitively defective, but they live in defective environments, which reduce their cognitive effectiveness for academic achievement compared to white, non-Latino students. Environmental deficit proponents suggest that interventions directed at the Latino and African American students' environments could be productive. Suggested interventions include improving living standards—specifically the diets and general health of pregnant women—and lifestyles, such as combating the disintegration of the traditional family and the proliferation of single parent and teenage-parent families who live below the poverty line.

Environmental deficit proponents argue strongly that poverty causes the majority of problems that Latinos and African Americans experience in schools, because poverty causes students to live in environments that disadvantage them. Therefore, a social network that combats the effects of poverty can serve to raise the academic achievement of Latinos and African Americans, who can then freely choose whatever life and career paths they want. As mentioned previously, early education for children is a potentially efficacious option. Educators might use this theory to blame the environment of their students, believing that since educators cannot do anything about the environment, why bother to strive for excellence in the classroom? In truth, educators can do something (and many have) about the environment of their classrooms. If educators are to succeed in a vision of equalizing, they must believe their efforts have the power to overcome home and community circumstances.

Unequal Access to Knowledge

This interpretation is perhaps the predominant one. Scholars such as W. E. B. Du Bois, George Sanchez, and Jane Addams posited that Latino and African American students do less well in academic work than white, non-Latino students because they also have less access to education. The quality and the quantity of education available to most Latino and African American students, this socioeconomic argument goes, are lower than that available to white, non-Latino students.

This interpretation was longstanding, coming to the fore in the 1950s. It formed the basis for arguments against segregated schooling. In the famous 1954 U.S. Supreme Court decision, *Brown v. Board of Education*, the court reasoned that "separate but equal" schools could not exist and that, in fact, racially separate schools deprived minority children of equal education opportunities even though the physical facilities and other tangible factors might be equal. In reality, the schools attended by minority children, almost always low-income children, were not equal to the schools attended by the majority of white children in the 1950s. Social and education critics contend (and almost no one would deny) that many modern schools are unequal. (The issue of equal educational opportunity is discussed further in this chapter under "Providing Equal Educational Opportunities.")

Cultural Incompatibility

The fourth interpretation is, in some respects, an extension of the third. This interpretation posits that minority students cannot benefit equally compared to majority students in schools where minority students experience cultural incongruity. In other words, minority students cannot benefit in schools where cultural compatibility is low or where the school culture of the majority is significantly different from—and locks out—the minority culture. The minority students are hampered if they cannot make a smooth transition from home culture to the school culture. (For more on culturally responsive teaching, see Gay, 2000.)

Equal education opportunity, the cultural incompatibility argument goes, cannot be achieved because the cultural mismatch between the student's home and school interferes with the transmission of knowledge. Sensitivity to diverse learners, regardless of the nature of that diversity, will assist educators in building on the students' prior experiences—cultural responsiveness—to create equal educational opportunities. (Equality of opportunity is discussed in the next chapter as equal benefit.)

The weakest of these four interpretations, in my view and in the view of most educators, is the first—cognitive deficit. Few serious scholars argue that the brains of individuals from different races are different from one another; that argument smacks of racial elitism and is not supported by scientific proof. The latter three interpretations assist by providing plausible explanations why African Americans and Latinos as groups are not as successful in school. Note that these are not rationalization for failure; it is perilous to assume students fail because of circumstances beyond the educator's control. In fact, many teachers have succeeded in spite of challenging circumstances. Teaching is not for the fainthearted. One must be committed to the idea teachers can make a difference in the lives of students.

The bottom line is that each student is unique and should be treated as such rather than assuming the outcome is already known, based on broad interpretations of group behavior or results. Talent exists everywhere.

The Impact of English Language Proficiency

Another achievement gap exists between English learners and native speakers of English. ELs are members of immigrant families who may speak one or more non-English languages. They speak English to varying degrees, or not at all, depending on the individual. Educators must understand that in any classroom, ELs are learning more than whatever subject is under study. Besides the content (math, history, science, and so on), they are learning the English language, which inhibits their ability at times to learn the content. On a deeper level, they are challenged to learn the culture that English reflects and the unspoken rules and dynamics of American classrooms.

Yet in the climate of the No Child Left Behind federal policy, schools are evaluated based on the test scores of their EL students. Any state, territory, or district receiving Title I funds must establish standards and a system of accountability to assess how the standards are met. All states are supposed to develop standards for English and mathematics achievement at all grade levels. The standards should address two areas: (1) content standards that describe at each grade level what students should know and be able to do and (2) performance standards of proficiency at each grade level, divided into partial proficiency, proficiency, and advanced.

Some states and major cities—New York, California, Chicago, Philadelphia—for example, have developed ESL standards. Others with insufficient numbers of English learners to justify statewide standards have adopted the *ESL Standards for Pre-K–12* provided by the professional organization Teachers of English to Speakers of Other Languages (TESOL, 1997).

School districts are now in the throes of aligning their curricula with state standards and developing pencil-and-paper tests to assess achievement. EL specialists must quickly familiarize themselves with their respective state and district's standards and tests.

Closing the achievement gap for English learners goes beyond EL specialists. Teachers in all classrooms should consider themselves teachers of English, and all teachers are expected to attend to the language needs of English learners. At first glance, this appears daunting. But teachers are not expected to teach elements of formal English functions, phrases, clauses, tenses, and so on. What they can do is link English literacy opportunities with the subject's contents, providing ELs practice with speaking, reading, and writing English. For example, most subjects contain key vocabularies and essential skills required for their performance. These can be written and translated, if needed, or they can serve as guides into the subject. Or an aide can assist with drills on the key words and the practice of essential skills.

A limited vocabulary in English makes reading difficult for ELs. Educators can compose a master list of vocabulary items of the classes' key terms. ELs should be taught the meaning of the words along with strategies for remembering them. During a lesson, the words should be highlighted as they appear in context. The teacher should ask the students to say the word and define it; students should be allowed to glance at the master list, if needed (Beck, McKeown, & Kucan, 2002; see also Nation, 2001).

Another suggestion is to use pre- and post-reading questions to serve as comprehension guides to the lesson (Echevarria, Vogt, & Short, 2004). A U.S. history lesson on westward expansion might pose pre-reading questions. As they read or engage in the lesson, students seek answers to such questions as: What was *manifest destiny?* How did the term get adopted? Who were some important people who pushed for manifest destiny? What areas of the U.S. did these people want to include in the United States? After the lesson, ELs team up with English speakers to answer the questions, restated as postreading questions. The students discuss the questions and finally agree on answers to write into their individual logs. If an individual disagrees with the team, that is also stated along with the individual's opinion of the answers.

All educators should become familiar with what is meant by "language competence." This overview of language competence (in any language) addresses the three areas of language ability I see as important:

1. *Grammatical competence* refers to knowledge of syntax, parts of speech, idiomatic, and phonological components of the language, and the traditional domains of language acquisition.

2. *Sociolinguistic competence* refers to knowledge of language usage rules regarding what is appropriate speech in different settings, with different topics, and with different speakers or registers of home talk, friend talk, and school talk.

3. *Strategic competence* refers to the capacity to apply the knowledge of grammatical and sociolinguistic competence while the person

is speaking or listening—translating and interpreting on an impromptu basis—in different social registers in an extended use of English with native speakers. Strategic competence is observed when a speaker can easily converse impromptu in formal and informal settings.

English-language proficiency can be stimulated via active learning. Following are some ideas for active approaches requiring ELs to think on their feet while translating and interpreting meaning.

Games

Word association games and games like charades can be very useful for translation and interpretation. Charades is especially effective because it relies heavily on nonverbal cues. The popular television game show *Jeopardy!* can be used to teach content in many subjects, such as history, science, and geography, to name a few. In addition, if the students are engaged in writing and playing the game, English literacy skills are also practiced. Other games, such as *Wheel of Fortune*, can be used similarly.

Role Playing

Role playing is a form of gaming. It is open ended, and its outcome is dependent on the students. Students are placed in a group; each is given a part to play for solving a problem such as, "Juan's grandmother needs to visit the doctor. She's frail but sees and walks well. She doesn't speak or read English." Someone in the group volunteers to be Juan. The others talk with Juan about how he might help his grandmother catch a bus (or subway), pay the toll, and otherwise make it to the doctor in time for her appointment. Another role-play activity could use the following prompt: "Help the grandmother compile a grocery list, using a sales ad from the newspaper. Then, help her at the grocery store with everything from finding items and asking for items to paying for them." The students dialogue in English with each other about how Juan might be of assistance. Juan may have to speak in Spanish to his grandmother. Encourage the students to consider all options, identify advantages and disadvantages, and then reach a realistic solution. The educator's task is to identify problems or conflicts that are nonthreatening to the students and are relevant to their experiences. The students may provide terrific ideas of their own.

Debating

Debating is also an excellent way to teach students to think on their feet. In the traditional debate format, there are two sides; each side has two individuals who argue for and against a proposition. For classroom language practice, the audience should also be involved as they will critique the debate. Provide the audience with a copy of the proposition with critique points. Each will be asked to decide which argument is the most convincing. The affirmative speaker goes first and may memorize a speech in favor of the proposition. (The negative speaker is allowed to take notes.) Then the negative speaker argues against the proposition. (The affirmative speaker is allowed to take notes.) This speech may also be memorized. Now comes the challenging part of the debate. Using notes, the affirmative speaker defends the affirmative position and attempts to disprove the negative's points. Then the negative speaker tries to disprove the affirmative position. When done, with the use of critique sheets, the audience speaks up, arguing why one side or the other was more convincing. Here's an example proposition: Fast food vendors should be required to label all the food they sell with the following: *Warning: Consumption of this food product can cause heart disease, stroke, and possibly death.*

The proposition requires the students to define the term *fast food* and to make an argument for and against the potential harm caused by the fast food. Both sides of the debate will have to conduct research (another literacy skill) in the ethics and legality of the proposition. Where does the matter of personal choice arise? Are individuals forced to eat fast food? Furthermore, students will be challenged to view the proposition from multiple perspectives (another literacy skill) to make arguments for and against the proposition. This particular proposition will require students to be at a higher level of English-language proficiency. For less mature students, a simpler proposition could be composed. Students may provide excellent ideas.

Practice

Require students to keep notes of everything important in class, such as the main idea of the lesson, key ideas studied, and new vocabulary. Allow students time to take notes even if they doodle. From time to time, read the student's notebook, and discuss it with him or her, asking for explanations about what's written or doodled. No red marks. No grades. Just talking about the subject with the student. The notebook is a good source for literacy development, study of the subject, and composition of word games, *Jeopardy!*, and so on. In elementary grades, ELs can write and illustrate their own books to be used in reading exercises, write and dramatize plays based on tales from their cultures, or write modern versions of old children's stories, such as Scieszka and Smith's book (1989) *The True Story of the 3 Little Pigs!*, which tells the old tale from the wolf's point of view.

The Impact of Gender

Achievement gaps in some subject areas still exist between boys and girls. The origins of those differences—whether they result from actual brain differences between the sexes, from children performing to perceived social expectations for gender roles, from teacher or system bias, or some combination of factors—are debated by scholars.

Consider the classic 1974 Maccoby and Jacklin study about the academic differences of boys and girls in elementary school. Maccoby and Jacklin reviewed the school records of more than 1,500 elementary school pupils and reported that girls and boys differed significantly in important ways. In the beginning grades, girls and boys performed comparably in all areas of the curriculum. However, the differences gradually widened with age and grade levels. During the first three years of elementary school, for example, girls performed equally well compared to boys in mathematics and visual-spatial activities. By sixth grade, however, girls were less assertive than boys but performed better verbally than boys, and boys performed better in mathematics and visual-spatial activities.

The NCES (2004) compiled longitudinal achievement data on school-age males and females, relying primarily on information generated by the National Assessment of Educational Progress. Gender differences in reading showed that females in grades 4, 8, and 12 consistently outperformed males, but there were no measurable increases in females' scores when 1992 data were compared to 2003. In science, trends have been slightly different compared to reading. Among grades 4 and 8, males scored higher than females on 2000 science assessments. The gap between males and females increased between 1996 and 2000 at grades 4 and 8, but there was no measurable difference in the size of the gap at grade 12. Interesting. The size of the gap increased in the lower grades, but leveled out at grade 12. Mathematics results are also interesting. Although a common perception is that males consistently outperform females in mathematics, the NAEP's mathematics scores have not shown this. In mathematics, the gap between average scale scores has been quite small and fluctuated only slightly between 1990 and 2003. In 2002, however, males made up a higher proportion of students taking AP exams in science and calculus. Males also obtained higher average scores on these examinations compared to females (NCES, 2004).

According to Maccoby and Jacklin (1974) and NCES (2004), in reading and mathematics females have held their own, but the science data show they have a way to go. Caution is necessary. Inferences are difficult to draw, given the wide range of time and the different research designs and databases in the two studies. Yet taken independently, one inference is apparent: each study reveals the subtlety of gender biases in the greater community and society. In short, the 1974 Maccoby and Jacklin study is still applicable, as corroborated by Koppelman and Goodhart (2005):

> In addition to declining test scores, girls encounter a curriculum that typically does not include much information on the achievement of women. . . . Educators still have to supplement textbooks with other instructional materials on women's achievements and women's issues to provide more equitable coverage. (p. 209)

Social factors weigh heavily for girls and boys. Even in the presence of nonbiased parents and teachers, boys and girls quickly absorb societal biases about what it means to be a boy or a girl. (See chapter 4 for more on this phenomenon.) Sex-differentiated socialization practices in the broader society may explain much of the gender differences in school performance. If we are not careful, both boys and girls will live down to gender-role stereotypes prevalent in society.

Teachers can counter gender-role stereotyping in the daily classroom routine and with selection of curriculum materials and textbooks. Think of gender-role stereotyping as shorthand for defining roles in terms of men's or women's work. For example, a fourth-grade teacher might ask some of the girls to help her tidy up the room in preparation for an invited guest speaker. Meanwhile, she may send some boys to the principal's office to greet and escort the guest to the classroom. (Message to children: men leave the house and take leadership, while women clean the house in preparation for the guests.)

As innocuous as this example may appear, it shows how teachers may unconsciously repeat chore assignments into a pattern that perpetuates gender-role stereotypes. Once aware of the behavior, teachers can simply rotate duties to allow both genders to assist with the various roles, neutralizing the stereotype. Here are some other suggestions:

- Examine your own attitudes about what you consider men's and women's work. Are you neutral? Or do you hold stereotypes, perhaps only in one facet? Be honest about your own attitudes.

- Check your own behavior. Do you favor one sex over the other as smarter, more obedient, more creative, and so on? If so, why? How can you readjust your bias?

- Provide positive role models by inviting successful individuals (both male and female) into your classroom. This is especially important in traditionally male-dominated professions such as science and mathematics.

- Select curriculum materials and textbooks that depict men and women fairly, showing females as well as men in active roles.

- Assign leadership roles to girls as often as to boys.

- Hold high expectations for all of your students, and assist in the achievement of them.

The Impact of Sexual Orientation

In addition to hidden or explicit gender biases, sexual orientation biases also persist. Huge numbers of students are affected; consider that between 8 and 14 million children are being reared in gay and lesbian homes. Homophobia and other sexual orientation issues also affect these youngsters (Baker, 2002). A good source for current information is the Gay, Lesbian and Straight Education Network (GLSEN). The network conducts and reports research about the experiences of lesbian, gay, bisexual, and transgender (LGBT) in schools, as in the following:

> The 2009 survey of 7,261 middle and high school students found that at school nearly 9 out of 10 LGBT students experienced harassment at school in the past year and nearly two-thirds felt unsafe because of their sexual orientation. Nearly a third of LGBT students skipped at least one day of school in the past month because of safety concerns. An analysis of National School Climate Survey data over 10 years showed that since 1999 there has been a decreasing trend in the frequency of hearing homophobic remarks; however, LGBT students' experiences with more severe forms of bullying and harassment may have remained relatively constant. (GLSEN, 2010, p. 1)

With gay and lesbian youth, or students whose parents are homosexual, teachers should focus on the individuals involved rather than relying on generalities.

Teachers can work to provide a safe learning environment free of harassment or abuse. Be on the alert for subtle and not-so-subtle references, such as "That's so gay," or "His father is a girly-man." Homophobia is deeply rooted in North American cultures and will not easily be stamped out. Yet there are schools and teachers who have worked to ensure an open environment in which a student's sexual orientation is not a condition for acceptance or rejection. Here are some suggestions:

- ❑ Examine your own attitudes toward homosexuality. Do you operate on the rule that all individuals, regardless of sexual orientation, are equally human, entitled to all the rights and privileges of being human? Do you hold stereotypes, or worse, prejudices? Be honest about your own attitudes. Seek competent, unbiased help for any doubts or misgivings you may have regarding homosexuality.

- ❑ Check your own behavior. Do you avoid the issue of homosexuality? Do you look the other way when students make snide remarks about a person's sexual orientation?

- ❑ Keep communications open with gay or lesbian parents by inviting them to school functions and involving them in your classroom.

- Provide leadership for any kind of support service that might be provided, such as "gay-straight" clubs or other alliances.

Providing gender and sexual orientation equity need not be onerous, although handling it requires finesse. Begin by assessing the context of your classroom and school (the neighborhoods and greater community) to better understand prevailing attitudes so you can develop a warm, inviting classroom open to diversity.

Providing Equal Educational Opportunities

My research on the evolution of teaching as a human behavioral pattern reveals that teaching children is one of the oldest and most important human activities. Prehistoric parents knew that the purpose of education was to teach their children what they needed to know to survive. They taught their children everything they knew. The parents were accountable for their teaching performance. If they failed to teach their children what was needed for survival, the children perished, along with the parents who didn't have anyone to take care of them when they were old. Everybody suffered from poor teaching. So parents had to decide:

- What's important to know?
- How should it be taught?
- Who should teach it?

The latter question was answered first; "what" and "how" followed. Teaching was divided by sex. Fathers taught their sons men's work; mothers taught their daughters women's work.

As cultures evolved and living became more complex and technical, master craftsmen and religious men (rarely women) assumed the role of teaching boys. Women continued to teach girls. For a very long time in Western cultures, education of boys was considered more important than girls because men's work was considered to be of greater value.

Education of girls is now taken seriously, which is an indicator of how cultures and perceptions about the social roles of men and women are also changing. For example, we now see female doctors practicing with male nurses, and female principals supervising male teachers.

Teaching children remains one of the primary parental tasks, but much of it has been delegated to schools. Teachers are put in a trust relationship with children. Parents trust teachers will educate their children on what's important to know as defined by state standards and school district curricula—and leave *how* they teach those standards and curricula to teachers. Those brave enough to teach assume an awesome responsibility with very high stakes.

Keep in mind that teachers are acting in place of the parents, and students have constitutional rights, such as freedom of expression, assembly, religion, and so on. Teachers also have the same rights. For teaching, the overarching consideration is the duty to provide each student an "equal educational opportunity." This duty has three dimensions: (1) safety, (2) equal access, and (3) equal benefit.

Safety

Schools and teachers should provide a safe environment conducive to learning. Classrooms should be safe places for children and adolescents. Safety is a fundamental principle that extends to intellectual and emotional well-being, not merely to physical. Of course, students should be kept safe from physical harm. Schools and classrooms must be in good physical condition, well lit, and ventilated. But schools and classrooms also must keep students safe from stress, abuse, or harassment that prevents them from learning or threatens their emotional security.

Safe classrooms allow students to be themselves within the conventions of behavior; however, those conventions of behavior may vary because of cultural diversity. Cultural awareness is crucial for the teacher and administrator, because such awareness can help them negotiate conventions and mediate conflicts that arise when so-called cultural norms are challenged.

For example, heterosexuality is considered the norm in many communities. Gay and lesbian students (or parents) may feel uncomfortable in schools in heterosexist communities. Administrators and teachers must provide these students and parents a safe environment, free of harassment and abuse. The educators must not hide their heads in a hole in the sand, hoping the "problem" will go away. The problem is not with the gay and lesbian students or parents. The problem is with prevailing attitudes intruding on the educators' responsibility to provide a safe learning environment. Ultimately, ignoring or avoiding the problem of heterosexism creates difficulties for the gay and lesbian students and parents.

Equal Access

Parallel dimensions to safety are equality of access and benefit. When most people think about equal educational opportunity, they think of the ideal; they think about ensuring that all students have equal access to good schools, high-quality instruction, and stimulating curricula—an open door to good schools and teachers. The struggle to provide such access has not been easy.

In the 1980s, a plethora of studies reported the major obstacle to provision of equal educational opportunities was the wealth of a school district, or the wealth of the community surrounding a school (Goodlad, 1984; Wilson, 1987). The studies consistently pointed to problems with resources. The richer districts and wealthier neighborhoods had better facilities, more experienced teachers, and higher graduation rates when compared to schools in low-income districts or neighborhoods, resulting in a disparity of educational quality. Responses to the studies were calls for educational reform at all levels, from local, state, and national governments. Although much has changed for the better since the 1980s, school districts everywhere still struggle to make equal access a reality. For current examples, see Archibald, 2006, and Fermanich & Kimball, 2002.

Equal Benefit

How can schools with diverse student populations ensure all students benefit equally from what the school has to offer? In other words, if a diverse student population is evidence that equal access has been achieved—all elements of the school are open to all students—then how can the school ensure that all students succeed on equal terms, that being part of a particular social class, linguistic, racial, or ethnic group does not affect whether or not success in school is achieved?

To answer these questions successfully takes a thorough understanding of the diversity issues I discussed in chapters 3 and 4 coupled with a finer sense of equality. Too often, accommodating differences—let's say, linguistic difference—gets translated into elitist terms. For example, when learners with limited English proficiency must tackle difficult texts, one approach can be to substitute simpler material—to dumb it down—rather than to improve the standard curriculum by adding alternative instruction strategies such as native-language translations and teaching methods that rely less on linguistic capability.

Dumbing down the curriculum does not accommodate diversity because it does not take equal benefit into account. This strategy is elitist when standards for students from middle- and upper-income families are higher than standards for students from lower-class families. Dumbing down can even be racist when students of one race are treated better—given a richer curriculum, for example—than those of another race.

Ability grouping and tracking often result in discrimination when the high- and middle-ability groups are provided with a rich, high-quality, college-bound curriculum, and the low groups are provided with a bare bones job-bound curriculum. Often the low tracks can be correlated to the non-white students' low socioeconomic status. This is why, in chapter 3, I propose universal goals for all students.

These are the treacherous waters of accommodation. Navigating them successfully takes both a keen understanding of diversity issues and a well-honed sense of equality of both access and benefit. But accommodation need not be treacherous. In fact, accommodation may be necessary for provision of equal opportunities.

The U.S. Supreme Court decision *Lau v. Nichols* (1974) is a good example of accommodation. The *Lau* decision shows how providing equal access changed into a more nuanced idea of providing equal "benefit" to students. Prior to *Lau*, immigrant and EL students were taught in English-only classrooms. Use of their home language was disallowed. English-only was strictly enforced to ensure students learned English. Students were often punished for speaking their home language. The *Lau* litigants provided evidence that many of these students fell behind their English-speaking peers and were more likely to drop out of school.

The *Lau* decision declared the English-only practice unfair. To paraphrase *Lau*, for students who do not understand English or are limited in English proficiency, equality of treatment in the classroom is not achieved solely by providing the same facilities, textbooks, teachers, and curricula in the same language. True, ELs had access to the same teachers, facilities, and curricula in the same language— English. But ELs could not benefit from that access. Consequently, the *Lau* ruling reasoned, access to knowledge is not equal in English-only classrooms. Special English language instruction is needed until ELs are able to participate fully in English-only classrooms. To ensure equal benefit, *Lau* permits the use of the home language while students are learning English.

Lau calls for special English instructional programs, but does not require any particular curriculum or approach. The specific program, with its attendant curriculum and approach, is chosen for ELs in consultation with parents and teachers. Research and experience have rendered several valid instructional approaches.

Bilingual education is used when a class of fifteen or more ELs speaks the same home language. School subjects are taught in the ELs' home language while they are learning English via special English-as-a-second-language lessons. Upon achieving English proficiency, the students are placed in classes where English is the sole language or transferred to a dual language program.

Dual language instruction is used when a class consists of a combination of English-only speaking students and bilingual and/or EL students. All the students do half of the coursework in English and half in the non-English language most spoken by the bilinguals and ELs. This approach is used to promote multicultural understandings and bilingualism in all the students.

Pull-out instruction literally pulls the EL out of the classroom for special lessons with other ELs during parts of the school day. Lessons are provided in English language skills for everyday conversations and for use in the student's English-only classes. Lessons about English may include study skills, listening, reading and writing exercises, and content-area vocabulary items of different subjects, such as science or geography terms. At other times in the day, ELs receive instruction with non-ELs in classes such as physical education, music, and art, and teachers are encouraged to use special techniques to assist the ELs.

Sheltered English is used when an entire class consists of ELs, who may or may not speak the same home language. Instruction is solely in English, targeting conversational speech, common vocabulary usages, and idiomatic expressions via slower speaking rates and constant repetition. This approach is often used in the upper grades when a class consists of immigrant and EL students who speak many different languages other than English.

English immersion is used when parents choose to enroll their EL children in classes taught solely in English, without any special assistance or instruction. Parents may select English immersion for any reason. It is recommended when the student is marginally EL, and the parents and teachers agree he or she is sufficiently proficient in English to require little or no special assistance.

This chapter explored the impact of sociocultural factors such as poverty, race and ethnicity, English proficiency, gender, and sexual orientation. These factors cause us to view students as members of groups rather than individuals. This perspective is acceptable only for purposes of better understanding the factors' impact on groups of students. The chapter also explored the policy of equality of educational opportunities, breaking it down into safety concerns and concerns about providing equal access and benefit to educational experiences. Our teaching attitude must always return to students as individuals deserving safe classrooms with equal access to educational experiences beneficial to each student.

Reflections

1. The chapter presents four theories (cognitive deficit, environmental deficit, unequal access, cultural incompatibility) to explain the academic gap that exists among African American,

Latino, and white students. Research and then report how educators in schools and universities have developed methods and techniques to lessen the gap with some populations, explaining which of the theories they may be using as a rationale.

2. I have provided much about the academic gap among African American, Latino, and white students. What about Native Americans? Research and report about the academic gap existent among Native Americans. Also research and report about methods and techniques developed to lessen the gap among Native Americans.

3. Here's an interesting phenomenon. Asian American students outpace African American, Latino, Native American, and white students in most indicators of academic achievement, such as high school graduation rates and overall grade point averages. The heritage of Asian Americans is vastly different than the so-called mainstream culture. Why do Asian American students do so well? Some scholars go so far as to dub the phenomenon "Asians—the model minority." Research and report on this phenomenon. What challenges do Asian Americans face? How do they address them so well? What can educators learn by understanding the phenomenon?

4. *Lau v. Nichols* was described as a good example of how educators can accommodate ELs. There are other laws that have catalyzed beneficial accommodations, namely the Individuals with Disabilities Education Act (IDEA) and Title IX of the Education Amendment of 1972. Research these laws. They are accessible online by name. Read the actual laws and then what educators have said about each. Study the accommodations required to benefit the students for whom each law is intended. IDEA's requirement of an individualized education plan (IEP) is an excellent model for individualization of instruction for all students. Also, with Title IX, schools have changed their policies, curricular, and extracurricular offerings to prevent sex discrimination.

seven

Teacher as Learning-Enabler

The adage "Give a man a fish, and he will eat for a day; teach a man to fish, and he will never go hungry" aptly captures the spirit of this chapter. Students may finish twelve grades and graduate, but are they viable individuals able to sustain a good life? Teachers should do more than help students pass a particular class or test. They should strive to facilitate the intellectual development of all their students. The aim is *empowerment* of students to think for themselves, construct knowledge, make meaning, and learn respect for themselves and others.

This chapter provides an overview of the changing roles teachers play; it contrasts constructivist and naturalistic education to clarify the changes to the roles. Then it summarizes the work of three noted scholars—Maria Montessori, John Dewey, and Paulo Freire—who strived to fuse the roles of teacher-as-giver and teacher-as-enabler.

Changing Role of the Teacher

Students learn through experiences, both planned and unplanned. Most societies do not leave the education of youth solely to unplanned, chance experiences but rather provide formal, planned experiences to transmit valued knowledge, skills, and beliefs, mainly through schools. Formal education assumes that knowledge brings power—that having knowledge leads directly to accomplishments. However, knowing something is one thing; *using* knowledge toward meaningful ends is another.

Teaching, then, should combine formal education and empowerment in an interactive teaching and learning pedagogy, the aims of which are active individuality and liberation from passive living. In the everyday world of the school and classroom, *empowerment* refers to helping students control and direct their feelings, thoughts, and actions to learn, to achieve socially constructive goals, and one hopes, to become lifelong learners. Empowering students, however, requires that educators must disempower themselves to an extent. By this I mean teachers must step back from their traditional role of knowledge-givers and instead adopt the role of learning-enablers.

The teacher as knowledge-giver teaches students codified knowledge: the facts and skills that have been identified by some authority (standards, state, district, teacher) as what a student must know. This process is inculcation of knowledge, the traditional role of teachers. The role remains relevant, but is challenged by the information explosion of our time—knowledge is exponentially expanding. How can students—and teachers—keep up? The teacher-as-enabler, by contrast, empowers students to construct meaning from experiences and codified knowledge and then act on that construction. Rather than learning "everything," the student learns how to learn: how to make sense of the vastly growing array of knowledge, ideas, and skills—not just how to fish, but how to change fishing techniques.

The knowledge-giver role serves to perpetuate cultures. Schools pass knowledge from one generation to the next; thus, the culture is replicated (albeit with some changes). But the capacity to pass on knowledge is necessarily limited. As our knowledge expands, schools must ensure the *best* knowledge is passed on and other information falls by the wayside. The selection of this best knowledge has been called the canon, that is, the compilation of knowledge into books. The knowledge explosion caused by ever-expanding technologies has changed how we use canons, however; permanent canons are no longer feasible. There is too much knowledge, and it is ever changing. Textbooks and other compilations of printed materials are constantly in need of revisions, much like this book in its third edition. Even as revisions are made, students have instant access to knowledge through electronic means. There is now more knowledge than can be put into any one canon, and the knowledge is constantly changing, making revisions a maddening, almost futile task. Furthermore, the old canons were not very diverse, mainly books written by men, excluding books by women and non-whites. Yet as we add new names to diversify the canons, others are cut to keep it manageable, causing contention as the topic— "What's important to know?"—is vigorously debated.

The task for teachers is not to merely teach a certain canon out of the many, but rather to assist students with the analysis, synthesis, and evaluation of all the knowledge available to them. This change in the teacher's role becomes clear when two views of teaching are contrasted: *constructivist* and *naturalistic* teaching.

Constructivist vs. Naturalistic Teaching

The teacher as learning-enabler is a constructivist view of teaching. Students actively construct meaning and understanding of reality by integrating and accommodating new information. Teachers help students scaffold from older information to newer information, or from prior experiences to newer ones. With constructivist teaching, the teacher moves from knowledge-giver to learning-enabler, or teacher-as-coach.

It is easy to see why this transition poses problems when one looks at the historical sense of teaching. *Teacher* equates to *teller*, one who tells or dispenses knowledge. In higher education, teachers are professors, those who profess or declare knowledge—often such knowledge is to be accepted, not disputed.

Given this historical sense of what teachers should do, it is not difficult to understand both societal and personal reluctance to shed the knowledge-giver role. For teachers trained in the traditional role, moving to the side to serve as an intellectual or academic coach seems like shirking responsibility. Parents reared in this method also sometimes wonder, "Why doesn't this teacher *teach?*"

It may help to clarify the constructivist position to say what constructivist teaching is not. It is not laissez-faire. The guide is on the side, not out of the room—or even on an equal level with the naïve student. The laissez-faire position, which is the true opposite of the knowledge-giver position, can be illustrated by a quick glance at the work of Jean-Jacques Rousseau.

In his 1762 book *Emile*, Rousseau (1979) described the education of a boy as laissez-faire, meaning that adults seldom interfered with or regulated the boy's education. Rousseau described the young child as a noble savage, a being full of pure thoughts and ideas but uncultivated to live in human society. According to Rousseau, if a child is left to his own intuitions, he or she will grow up to be a good person. If a child is corrupted by society in the guise of formal education, then he or she will take on society's ills. Therefore, Rousseau reasoned, children should experience a "natural education," in which adults watch over the child, but do not intrude on the child's quest for knowledge. This approach would prevent corruption by adults.

Such natural education has had some appeal, though it strikes me as impractical, and few education theorists have taken the notion as far as Rousseau. Friedrich Froebel (1782–1852) adopted aspects of natural education in his concept of the *kindergarten* (Froebel, 1977), the children's garden, where children were free to explore, following their curiosities within a structured environment or what I call "structured play." Today, some kindergartens are shifting to an emphasis on academic preparation for first grade. I have mixed feelings about that shift. Kindergarten, as originally adopted by public schools in the United States, stressed socialization; structured play was used to teach preschoolers to get along with each other and to grow accustomed to the classroom routine. Structured play is not frivolous. It is carefully planned to lay the foundation for the formation of important behaviors. In the words of the preeminent educator Maria Montessori (1972):

> The child who has never learned to work by himself, to set goals for his own acts, or to be the master of his own force of will, is recognized in the adult who lets others guide him. (p. 20)

Students need to develop the ability to think and do for themselves—to know when to lead and when to follow. In this book, I raise autonomy and self-discipline to the level of a goal of universal education. Students do not automatically learn autonomy and self-discipline. In the past, the foundation was laid in kindergarten via structured play. Then in the remaining grades, socialization takes a second emphasis over academics. My concern is that the shift toward academics in kindergarten may shortchange socialization of children (and our society) by depriving preschoolers of this early opportunity to learn respect for the rights of others and develop self-discipline.

Fusion of Teaching Roles

Natural or laissez-faire education does not meet one premise of constructivist teaching: it omits adult assistance. The teacher is neither the sage on stage nor the guide on the side. Constructivist theory allows teachers to act as a coach or facilitator of learning for students. The role of the teacher includes both didactic, direct instruction and coaching, or indirect instruction.

The sports coach is an appropriate model. Coaches of sports use direct instruction to impart important knowledge. Football players call such direct teaching "skull sessions." Learners incorporate such information into their own knowledge base, modifying existing understandings to create new meaning. Then coaches move aside and allow learners to apply and practice those new understandings, providing correction and advice as needed.

For example, it would be a foolish waste of time to expect students simply to discover the rules of fishing: how to string a line, bait a hook, cast, and so on. This knowledge is most efficiently conveyed through direct instruction. But learning directly how to string a line, bait a hook, and cast is only the beginning. Students also must learn how to watch the bobber and set a hook when a fish nibbles the bait. In short, students need to learn to fish in practical ways (physically) after they have learned how to fish theoretically (rules and procedures). Actually *fishing* requires the teacher to get out of the way—to teach indirectly by coaching from the banks of the river or lake.

Coaching is not confined to sports. In fact, teachers coach much of the time even though they may not think of themselves as coaches. This coaching or facilitative teaching allows and encourages the student to become self-directed. The student-as-player becomes active, thus gaining critical consciousness, the capacity to make decisions and have thoughts and feelings that are not dictated by the teacher. This manner of instruction is well suited to teaching for diversity, because it provides a framework for instruction within which students are more likely to be able to be themselves, to feel safe in being themselves, and to derive equal benefit from instruction to which they and their peers have access.

In summary, the role of the teacher is shifting to a fusion of the sage on the stage with a guide on the side. When should a teacher give, and when should he or she guide? The decision requires artistic judgment. Three pioneering figures in the movement to fuse knowledge giving with learning enabling have explored this question: Maria Montessori, John Dewey, and Paulo Freire.

Maria Montessori

Maria Montessori (1870–1952) was born in Italy, trained as a doctor, and pursued her work as an educator in Italy where women were not allowed to practice medicine, during her lifetime. She turned to education of Italian orphans—boys who were considered uneducable (Montessori, 1917). Using the traditional teacher-as-teller approach, she soon discovered that the orphans did not understand her because of their experiential backgrounds. She began experimenting with the use of manipulative objects and hands-on lessons and eventually came to the conclusion that learning is an organic process carried out by individuals, and the role of the teacher-as-facilitator is to release each student's potential. In other words, learners are like artists, constructing meaning as they go along. They develop skills at their own pace as they integrate new knowledge. They are then enabled to think and do for themselves.

Her hands-on approaches worked with the illiterate, orphan boys who were considered uneducable by Italian authorities. Because of her success, Montessori was allowed to expand her school into an educational system for the poor in Italy. Before long, she was recognized as a leading educator, and various other governments hired her to establish her system in their countries. Her approaches were also adopted in the United States by private schools. Most public schools did not adopt her methodology. I am not sure why, although because of that, her methods are now available primarily to students from affluent backgrounds in private schools.

John Dewey

John Dewey (1859–1952) opposed teaching that fragmented knowledge into subject areas, arguing that the subject areas that made sense to adults did not necessarily make sense to young children (Dewey,

1902). Young minds, Dewey suggested, do not fragment reality into discrete, abstract subjects. Rather, he argued, young minds deal with the immediate: children learn holistically from experiences and by doing, although at times they need to be told, that is, they require direct instruction.

John Dewey proposed pedagogy that would enable individuals to live in a democratic society by developing their reflective habits of mind. Dewey suggested alternative ways for pupils to construct their own meaning and interpretations of the knowledge codified by authorities, rather than via the memorization often required in formal education. His methods included (1) supposition: formulation of a hypothesis, gathering and analyzing data, and drawing inferences, and (2) reflection: identification of a problem, analysis of its causes, and presentation of solutions.

Like Maria Montessori, Dewey drew on his own experiences—in his case, from the laboratory school at the University of Chicago, which he operated in the first decades of the 20th century to experiment with his theories. Teachers in the school developed problem-solving lessons, experiments, and projects that were based not on a narrow canon, but on the curiosity and interests of their students. This grounding led to the development of the progressive education movement. By the 1930s, however, the movement had lost steam and was being criticized for its lack of performance standards. Even Dewey was critical of interpreters of the movement and his pioneering work (Dewey, 1938).

Paulo Freire

The progressive spirit permutated and was revived in the late 1960s and 1970s. Paulo Freire (1921–1997) was born in Brazil and was concerned with oppressed peoples—for whom, he argued, education was not a liberating force. In Freire's Pedagogy of the Oppressed (1970), he challenged the knowledge-giver philosophy by calling it the "banking method" of teaching: teachers deposit knowledge in the heads of their students, but the knowledge remains the property of the teacher. The students do not own the knowledge because they have not made it. Freire contended that the banking method serves to oppress students because they are given the thoughts and feelings of others without being allowed to develop thoughts and feelings of their own. They are dependent on teachers to deposit new knowledge. They are enslaved rather than freed to think and do for themselves.

Freire worked as a teacher in Brazil and other Latin American countries, where he experienced firsthand the oppressive nature of conventional, knowledge-giving instruction. He saw how schools treated ethnic minority peasants, compelling them to learn the state language and to adopt mainstream cultural values—and to discard their native language and culture, to assimilate into the so-called mainstream. Many such students left school and remained illiterate rather than give up their home culture.

Under such regimes, Freire suggested, pupils are indoctrinated and not encouraged to think independently or to define their individuality and understand their subjugated positions in society. They are dominated by the consciousness of the ruling class. Freire proposed replacing the banking method with assisting individuals to develop what he called *critical consciousness*—in other words, the capacity to understand one's own reality, make meaning about that reality, and transform that reality.

Freire was determined to treat students differently. Through question-and-answer strategies, he drew out his students and discovered their experiences and interests. On this basis, over the course of six months, his once-illiterate students were reading and writing in their native language; this allowed them to develop knowledge (to make meaning) in terms that made sense to them. Once students could think for themselves, then they could benefit from mainstream schooling if they chose to do so. To Freire, this liberation of mind was the keystone of schooling (Freire, 1970).

In times of political oppression, however, governments seldom want people to think for themselves, particularly if those people are ethnic minority peasants. Freire was exiled from his native land for teaching peasants to think for themselves. The same attitude once prevailed in the U.S. South; during the antebellum period, it was illegal to teach slaves to read and write. Slave-state authorities feared that literate slaves—slaves who could think for themselves—would be more likely to rebel against their masters. And they often did.

Education should be a liberating force in the lives of students, and teachers should strive to empower students to think and do for themselves. Rather than be knowledge-givers, teachers should be learning-enablers, fusing knowledge-giving and guiding. There is a time and place for guiding and for giving. As students learn to construct meaning, they become their own teachers.

Reflections

1. Two teaching metaphors are woven throughout this chapter:

    a. "Give a man a fish, and he will eat for a day. Teach a man to fish, and he will never go hungry."

    b. "Rather than a sage on stage, be a guide on the side."

    Explain how they are similar and how they differ. Then discuss examples of both metaphors you have seen in action in day-to-day affairs outside the classroom.

2. This chapter describes the teacher-as-enabler. Reflect on other teaching metaphors, and describe their focus. Is it on the teacher? The student? What roles do the teacher and student play in the metaphor? Following are some metaphors; you may think of others:

    a. Teacher as shepherd

    b. Teacher as gardener

    c. Teacher as zookeeper

3. Educators have to decide when to give knowledge and when to guide students in pursuit of knowledge. Thoughtful scholars and practitioners, including the following, have given much

thought to fusing the two into an overall teaching strategy. Form a reading circle, select reading assignments, and then share knowledge on the writers' approaches: Dewey on the progressive education movement, Montessori on her approaches, Freire on literacy instruction, Aston-Warner on her approaches with Maori children in New Zealand, and Sapon-Shevin on contemporary approaches for working with diverse student populations:

- ❏ John Dewey (1938), *Experience and Education*

- ❏ Paulo Freire (1970), *Pedagogy of the Oppressed*

- ❏ Maria Montessori (1917), *The Advanced Montessori Method*

- ❏ Mara Sapon-Shevin (2010), *Because We Can Change the World*

- ❏ Sylvia Ashton-Warner (1963), *Teacher*

eight

Linking Goals and Instructional Strategies

Having laid a foundation for instruction that accommodates diversity, I now turn to specific instructional strategies that are aligned with the goals of universal education:

- ❏ Fostering learning autonomy via self-discipline

- ❏ Fostering intellectual effectiveness via critical thinking

- ❏ Fostering cultural efficacy via cross-cultural interaction

While I will treat these areas separately, it should be clear they overlap and interconnect. The strategies are intended to provide teachers a way to weave their role as learning-enabler into the fabric of instruction.

Learning Autonomy via Self-Discipline

As previous chapters have discussed, successful living in a free society requires individuals willing and able to think and do for themselves. In school, students should be willing and able to take responsibility for learning. Most students learn autonomy and self-discipline at home and in the early grades, but some do not. Teachers can facilitate this development by enabling students to manage their own behavior.

Sometimes self-discipline becomes a heightened concern when teachers encourage students to think and act on their own initiatives. This is true in a mostly homogeneous classroom; it becomes even more of a factor when the class makeup is highly diverse. How can teachers establish good behavior without becoming too authoritarian and directive? And how can teachers maintain good classroom behavior, encourage autonomy, and deal positively with cultural differences simultaneously?

The answer to all of these questions lies mainly in helping students learn to balance autonomy with self-discipline. Autonomy carries the notion of freedom—freedom to learn, freedom to choose subjects and methods of study, and so on. However, no freedom is absolute. Autonomy must be tempered by self-discipline, which means that students choose what and how to learn within certain limits. They have to work within the norms of the classroom. Low self-discipline can lead to inappropriate behavior, a management problem both for the teacher—because the student's actions may interfere with other students' learning or the teacher's ability to teach—and for the student, whose own ability to learn is diminished. One response to low self-discipline is to impose greater external control. This response is likely to be effective only in the short term. The better response—and the only response likely to succeed in the long term—is to investigate the source of the student's low sense of self-discipline and to work to solve that problem.

Part of self-discipline is developed through teacher direction. Within facilitative teaching, certain elements will be convergent: teacher-determined goals, direct instruction, and so on. Students learn a measure of self-discipline through observing the teacher's examples. Another part of self-discipline comes from external expectations—from parents, the community, and society in general.

The key part of the development of self-discipline is the student's sense of self. Belief that an individual can produce a change in him- or herself or others, is what psychologists call *self-efficacy*. Belief in the ability to control one's actions is a strong part of self-discipline—and it goes hand-in-hand with feelings of autonomy as a learner.

A student's sense of self-efficacy can be encouraged or discouraged by the responses of the teacher and peers to the student's appearance, speech, family background, religious beliefs, and so on. In short, the student's sense of self is linked to his or her feelings of acceptance: self-acceptance, peer acceptance, acceptance by parents and significant others, teacher acceptance, and acceptance by the world in general.

Because self-efficacy is built on beliefs about what one can do—in other words, the effect one can produce—teachers can aid self-efficacy by helping students (1) set realistic goals and standards, (2) direct behavior toward achievement, (3) assess achievement and adjust direction, and (4) redirect goals based on achievement.

Set Realistic Goals and Standards

Maria is a student in a swimming class. She wants to be an Olympic swimmer, but she only started swimming at the age of fifteen. Although it is unlikely that Maria will ever qualify for the Olympic team, it would be unfair to dismiss her dream ("Oh, Maria, you'll never make it"). On the other hand, it would be equally unfair to be mindlessly optimistic ("Maria, you can do anything you put your mind to"). Maria needs help setting realistic goals. For example, a reasonable goal might be for her to try out for the swim team at school or at the local swim club. Realistic goals and standards are more likely than "pie in the sky" goals to lead to solid achievements that build the student's sense of self-efficacy. In Maria's case, realistic goals that are met may lead to a lifelong love of swimming, a college swimming scholarship, and yes, perhaps even the Olympics.

Direct Behavior Toward Achievement

Many students set goals for themselves but then fail to follow through. Achievement takes action; it takes doing, not just thinking. When Maria sets her goal as joining the local swim club, she also needs to be guided to think about how that goal can be achieved. Will it require a certain amount of practice? When will she do that practice? Will her practice be enhanced by changes in diet or sleeping patterns? To build self-efficacy, Maria may need guidance to discover the details that will best chart her path to goal achievement. Facilitative teaching can be used to help Maria make the necessary discoveries and to learn how to think about goal fulfillment in proactive ways in other situations.

Assess Achievement and Adjust Direction

Maria has difficulty with the butterfly-stroke lap of a swim relay. She feels like a failure. To distinguish herself and get on the swim team, she must improve her butterfly stroke. The thoughtful teacher (in the role of coach) will recognize—and help Maria recognize—that achievement is earned in stages. Maria is assessing her own achievement when she recognizes that she needs to work on her butterfly stroke, but her assumption of failure is unproductive. The teacher needs to help her understand that this need is not a failure—nor is *she* a failure because she has this need. Improving the butterfly stroke is a realistic goal. Once Maria realizes this, she can adjust the direction of her efforts by defining (for herself) the steps it will take to achieve her goal of improving her butterfly stroke.

Redirect Goals Based on Achievement

What happens after a goal is achieved? The easy answer is—set another goal. Indeed, achievement of one goal often reveals a new goal. Maria realizes her goal of making the swim team, an achievement to be celebrated. But the achievement also reveals another goal: to be the best swimmer (or one of the best) on the team, for example.

By engaging in this four-step process with students, teachers can help students balance autonomy with self-control. Because the process gives students a sense of direction they can take, it fosters stronger feelings of self-efficacy. Following are some general suggestions for taking these steps into the academic environment:

- Ask students to compile a list of skills they want to master. Help them prioritize their list.
- Help students develop goals related to their priorities; break large goals into more workable pieces.
- Work with students to develop action plans that will guide them toward achievement of their goals. Set up timelines for achievement.
- Encourage students to reexamine their goals periodically, assess their progress, and readjust their goals as needed.
- Celebrate goal attainment, and help students base new goals on goals they have already achieved.

Students with low self-efficacy will present the greatest behavioral management challenges. Insecurity about one's value and feelings of alienation and rejection can lie behind some students' need to act out, defy authority, or, conversely, withdraw from social interaction. Students who perceive themselves as different in the negative sense are more likely to express feelings of low self-efficacy than students who consider themselves to be part of the school and classroom community.

Intellectual Effectiveness via Critical Thinking

Access to knowledge from various cultures and sources is a necessity, but what to make of that knowledge is also important. Making sense of knowledge and evaluating your own thought processes are possible through critical thinking, essential to a 21st century education:

> Even if all students earned a high school diploma and mastered tradi-
> tional academic subjects, they 'still' would be ill prepared. . . . today,
> a different set of skills—21st century skills—increasingly powers the
> wealth of nations. Skills that support innovation, including creativity,
> critical thinking, and problem solving, are in increasing demand. (Kay,
> 2010, p. xviii)

Widespread support for teaching critical thinking skills exists. Pickering (2010) reveals such support by citing President Obama's 2008 *Plan for American Leadership in Space,* which called for K–12 education to teach higher-order critical thinking skills. I believe *critical thinking* refers to the centrality of thinking about an issue, problem, or question of concern. It does not mean disapproval or negativity.

Similarly, support for teaching critical thinking skills exists, but how to teach the skills is another matter. Teachers and students need guidance to analyze, synthesize, and evaluate the mass of information available to them. Pickering (2010) makes the case for directly teaching critical thinking skills. Citing three different studies, she shows how students' academic achievement is increased on standardized tests when teachers required in-depth study and critical thinking applications within the context of the subjects taught.

Pickering goes on to describe a major challenge for teachers—the broad spectrum of definitions and approaches about critical thinking. Which definitions and approaches should teachers select? She recommends that educators narrow their focus, that is, identify and teach the thinking skills needed for an in-depth study of the subjects they teach. I like her recommendation. It empowers teachers to identify and teach critical thinking within their daily routine.

In the spirit of narrowing focus, I offer some basic ideas in the following paragraphs as a means to foster critical thinking among students. The key to understanding the significance of critical thinking in education is to understand the significance of critical thinking in learning.

Critical thinking can play a part in learning in two ways. The first is when students construct in their own minds the ideas, concepts, and principles intrinsic in the subject matter they are studying. The second is when students use those ideas, concepts, and principles. Teachers play a very important part. (For instance, in chapter 7, the teacher's role was described as teacher as a learning-enabler.) Teachers guide students through the learning process by cultivating reflections in the students, that is, teachers guide the students by asking them to reflect on their own thinking.

I believe critical thinking at its most basic level is the act of reflecting on one's own thoughts to determine the extent of their veracity, that is, to what extent are my thoughts accurate or truthful? With this notion of critical thinking, I am referring to the learning process that involves doubt and resolution, what John Dewey called *reflection*:

> Reflective thinking . . . involves (1) a state of doubt, hesitation, perplexity, mental difficulty, in which thinking originates, and (2) an act of searching, hunting, inquiring to find material that will solve the doubt, settle and dispose of the perplexity. (1933, p. 12)

Use the Three-Question Method

Dewey's definition implicitly provides a method to involve students in critical thinking. Using this method, teacher and student engage in a dialogue with the teacher serving as a guide. The method can be stated as three questions:

1. What do I want to know?
2. How can I find the answers?
3. How do I know whether the answers are any good?

Breaking down the definition into parts provides a way for students to think critically about a subject. First, Dewey's definition states that thinking originates in a "state of doubt, hesitation, perplexity, mental difficulty" (1933, p. 12). This is the beginning of the critical thinking process. The student may be puzzled, confused, or curious about something being taught, which suggests the first inquiry question: what do I want to know? This is the first step for inquiry. It requires definition and challenges students to refine their thinking processes. It allows them to focus more clearly on what it is they want to know.

In dialogue with their teacher and other students, they answer the question by explicitly defining their state of doubt or hesitation.

Now that their focus is clearer, they are able to seek out answers—the second step for inquiry. As in Dewey's definition, seeking answers is an "act of searching, hunting, inquiring to find material that will solve the doubt, settle and dispose of the perplexity" (1933, p. 12). In conjunction with the teacher, students consider different means to get answers, pointing to the question: how can I find the answers? This question addresses the practical means students will use to get answers. Students have various ways of getting answers through epistemologies—ways of knowing. For example, students might use the opinions of experts (authority epistemology) to get answers.

After gathering information from the experts, the students now have answers. This process points to the third inquiry question: how do I know whether the answers are any good? This is the stage for evaluation of the information to determine validity. Again teacher and student engage in a dialogue, the teacher serving as a guide about how to assess whether or not the answers are valid. The teacher and student can make decisions about the next steps about the inquiry, such as to conclude the study, conduct more research, or make an oral or written report about the findings to others. Simply put, the three-question method is a conversation between teacher and student. The teacher guides the student, engaging the student in some area of critical thinking, such as analysis, synthesis, or evaluation. He or she works in tandem with the student, assisting with the thinking process involved in each step.

Implicit in Dewey's definition is that reflective thinking involves shedding preconceptions and, if you will, prejudices. This is an important concept in teaching for diversity, because ingrained preconceptions and prejudices about individuals who are different get in the way of clear thinking.

Another way to view critical thinking is to look at solving problems. When humans attempt to solve problems, critical thinkers usually go about the task by using divergent or convergent strategies, as discussed previously. *Divergent* thinking refers to creating new ideas and devising options. Brainstorming and free association are divergent thinking strategies. By creating ideas freely, a solution (or more than one solution) may be found for a problem. *Convergent* thinking, in contrast, refers to assessing existing ideas, making judgments, and narrowing options. Weighing pros and cons and looking behind the ideas to find their merits are strategies of convergent thinking. Divergent and convergent strategies often are used in tandem to solve problems.

Teach Epistemologies

Ultimately, critical thinking is about arriving at judgments. Whether approaching the three inquiry steps with a convergent or divergent strategy, they can be managed with one or more of commonly used *epistemologies*, or methods of knowing: (1) authority—relying on expert opinion, (2) reason—applying logic, (3) experimentation—testing theories or possible solutions, and (4) observation—relying on the senses. We use these methods for knowing, or getting answers, in everyday living, although we rarely think of them as epistemologies. When we're perplexed, we go through a process of deriving answers till we find them or give up.

What follows is a brief description of the four epistemologies commonly used by people to solve everyday problems. After the brief descriptions, a scenario is provided that demonstrates how the epistemologies are used interactively. By this scenario, a teacher can understand how the epistemologies might be applied in the classroom.

Authority

Experts answer questions by providing their opinions. The opinions are derived from a host of sources, including other epistemologies, such as reasoning and logic, experimentation, and observation. Whether or not the opinions are correct is a matter of interpretation and trust. One must evaluate the opinions to determine their veracity—or one can take them on faith. One trusts experts, yet authority is never infallible. Therefore, it is wise to verify the expert's opinions by getting a second opinion, or a third. Even then, expert opinion may be insufficient. One needs to use other epistemologies.

Reasoning and Logic

This epistemology is excellent for getting a theoretical or hypothetical answer. Reasoning and logic can render an answer that is true within the bounds of the reasoning and logic used. For example, if I wonder whether I have enough gas to get to another town, I can apply a mathematical formula. I have to travel sixty miles. My car has three gallons of gasoline in it; the car gets twenty miles to the gallon. Reason and logic say, yes, I will make it to the other town. In theory, the answer is correct. But will the answer be correct in reality? If the town sixty miles away lies downhill, I may have more than enough gas. But if it lies uphill, I may not have enough gas. And what about wind? A head wind would also lower my car's gas mileage; a tailwind could raise it. Reasoning and logic may provide an answer that is good enough for specific purposes. Other times, one can use reason and logic to build a theory that can be tested through experimentation and observation.

Experimentation and Observation

Experimentation is used to test a theory in order to support or disprove it. An experiment or test can be carried out to answer a question or investigate a problem. Observation, gathering information that we see, hear, feel, and so on, is the most common form of scientific inquiry and is often used with experimentation to investigate ideas or theories. With the experimentation epistemology, one states a proposition—an idea or theory—then devises a test or means to examine the proposition's veracity, taking time then to observe the entire process carefully. The procedures used to test the proposition are clearly stated so others can examine it, and if desired, replicate the study. Replication can serve to verify the original study, or it may reveal difficulties with the study's answers. The results are analyzed, a conclusion is drawn, and results are communicated through research papers or oral reports. (In the Reflections section, a handbook on experimentation is recommended for teachers seeking ideas for experiments.)

Teach Pitfalls of Critical Thinking to Avoid

Following are some informative critical thinking pitfalls and habits of thought:

- ❑ Bias—One's perceptions form the primary filters for interpreting reality. Bias and prejudices narrow the lens of perception to preconceived ideas. Biased perception is selective and blocks the consideration of new ideas.

> ❏ Stereotyping—When bias is generalized to a group (type), then misconceptions are perpetuated, and new information is closed out. Stereotyping obscures accurate perceptions of individuals within the group.

> ❏ Absolutes—Absolutes exist in the abstract, rarely in the concrete. Rigid, categorical thinking (either/or, black or white) obscures nuances of meaning and blocks out essential ambiguity.

Effective critical thinkers: (1) ask penetrating questions that go beyond biases and stereotypes; (2) defer judgment until all possibilities have been considered and all information gathered; (3) consider a wide array of options, ideas, and solutions, examining them with sensitivity to cultural issues; and (4) look for connections between new and existing knowledge and understanding, knowing that such connections are how meaning is constructed.

In this section I have touched on critical-thinking issues that have a particular bearing on teaching for diversity. Clearly, critical thinking could be—and has been—the subject of entire books (Pickering, 2010). My goal has been simply to provide a starting point for engaging students in critical thinking—teaching students to think and do for themselves—as a key component of teaching for diversity.

Cultural Efficacy via Cross-Cultural Interaction

This section focuses on enabling students to relate to others with whom they do not share cultures. My intent here is to provide a starting point for thinking about teaching diverse students how to get along and, indeed, how to benefit from interactions with one another so they can function in a diverse world.

What does it take for students to function effectively outside their home cultures? The facile answer is this: become less provincial and more cosmopolitan. But individuals who are like-minded—for example, of the same ethnicity or the same sex—tend to coalesce. (See chapter 5 for the discussion on ethnocentrism and mild group pride associated with ethnic group cohesiveness.)

One objective of cross-cultural interaction is to foster recognition and value for legitimate group pride, in terms of both one's own cultural group and of other groups. That recognition and value must begin with teachers and administrators before it can be transmitted to students. Such recognition often starts with seeing one's own prejudices. I recall a colleague saying, "I don't notice that my new students are black or white. To me, they are all as white as I am." He was sincerely trying to be colorblind, trying to treat all students equally without regard to race, but he didn't realize his unwitting prejudice. "They are as white as I am" implied that being white is superior, or that something is wrong about being black.

Equal education is not about becoming colorblind but about treating all students fairly, which includes extending equal regard for each student's culture. Effective cross-cultural interaction must start with learning about different cultures. Thus for educators and their students, cross-cultural interaction must begin with openness. Students must be encouraged to share their culture, if they wish, and explore other cultures. Following are three general strategies for enhancing awareness and fostering communication and cross-cultural interaction: (1) exposure and cooperation, (2) language study, and (3) cultural interaction through the Internet. (Teaching about a culture is described in chapter 9.)

Exposure and Cooperation

Students need to learn about one another's cultures in both formal and informal ways. They can learn directly about other cultures through research, reading, and other formal classroom activities. Teachers can structure student exchanges and cultural field trips. They can invite guests into the classroom. Such basic knowledge-building strategies are most helpful when they encompass not only the cultural representation of the classroom but also cultures not represented in the classroom. This is especially true in schools and classrooms that are largely homogeneous, where teachers may not feel any particular urgency to promote cross-cultural awareness and interaction. However, students in homogenous classrooms are going to live in a world that is multicultural. In addition, these classes are most likely multiethnic; an all-Asian classroom does not mean all the students share the same ethnicity. These students need to be able to function across cultures as much as those who attend heterogeneous classrooms.

Informal learning comes about from casual contact. Working together in cooperative groups, for example, is a way for students to come into natural contact with peers from other cultures and to learn about those cultures indirectly. This is an application of my contact thesis, described in chapter 5, that posits if individuals work together as equals, they will develop bonds of respect and friendship. Many teachers who have applied this thesis—in classrooms composed of students who differed by race, social class, academic achievement, and sex—have found that the thesis holds true.

Language Study

Studying a foreign language is another way for students (and teachers) to learn about other cultures. By studying another language, one also learns much about one's own language. This is true in terms of the cultures of the target language, but it also is true in terms of general language principles. Studying a foreign language helps students become aware of language-bound differences among peoples and cultures. For example, in English, one says, "The clock is running." One cannot say that in Spanish. The comparable expression in Spanish is, "The clock is *walking*." What does this say about a cultural sense of time?

The ideal situation is to be immersed in a language study, but that is often not practical. Students need not study a language in depth to benefit. Many teachers can learn how to provide an introduction to a variety of languages that will help students gain a stronger sense of other cultures along with a deeper understanding of how language and culture interconnect.

Cultural Interaction Through the Internet

The Internet is a worldwide network of repositories containing a multitude of sources, such as virtual libraries, reference works, journals, collections, government reports, and numerous other informational resources, instantly accessible at the click of a mouse.

The web provides vast information. Teachers must address the challenges of how to make sense of the information and use it ethically.

They can use the web to develop an understanding of cross-cultural topics and issues and to assist their students in assessing the quality of the sources and information. Don't give too much credence to information and sources found online. "It must be true; I read it on the Internet" does not always hold water. Anybody with access to the Internet can upload information.

Assessing online information for authenticity, accuracy, and bias is a necessary exercise in critical thinking, especially if the Internet is to serve educative purposes. Web sources are much like any other. They may contain biases, errors, or false statements couched in scientific or scholarly language. Teachers can help students apply the critical-thinking approaches described previously to make good judgments about the web sources and information.

Helping students connect with students in other locations can also make for rewarding cross-cultural interactions. A strategy that springs immediately to mind is the setting up of electronic pen-pal exchanges. Teachers have assisted students with pen pals in other countries for many years. For a new twist, they can use the Internet for such exchanges. Check out the website ePals (www.epals.com), which claims to be the Internet's largest global community. Teachers need not enroll in a commercial website, however. They can check with curriculum directors or their state department of public education to find noncommercial connections.

Conclusion

I have tried to demonstrate in this chapter that teachers can accommodate diversity while addressing the three goals of universal education. Some necessary preconditions are worth reiterating. First, teachers must take into account safety and equality issues. Schools must be places where students feel safe—physically, intellectually, and emotionally. Equality is more than mere access; students need the tools to benefit equally from the education offered to them.

Second, instructional strategies that accommodate diversity must be grounded in sound theory. School experiences should assist students in learning about themselves and about others. In prior chapters, I mentioned the works of Dewey, Freire, and Montessori. Numerous other theorists, researchers, and practitioners have offered bases for thinking about multiculturalism and how to help students discover self-awareness—who they are individually and culturally—and awareness of others—connections with individuals from other cultures.

Third, I have suggested the teacher's role is less that of the sage on the stage and more that of a guide on the side. The transition from knowledge-giver to learning-enabler may be difficult for some teachers to accept and even harder to implement. I hope the goals and strategies in this chapter assist teachers in making the synthesis between the two roles.

Reflections

1. This chapter presented instructional strategies as a means to achieve universal goals of education. How would you make use of the strategies? Develop a plan about how you would use the goals and strategies while teaching within one or more subjects. Then compare and contrast your plan with others. Examine how these goals and strategies can be incorporated within the subject matter taught in any given course and grade level.

2. Have some fun with critical thinking exercises. Google "brain teasers" and then pull up several websites, such as www .azkidsnet.com/brainteasers.htm or www.brainbashers.com. You'll find an array of riddles, optical illusions, puzzles, and logic games. Develop lesson plans with the materials and try them out with students.

3. One need not be a science major to conduct experiments in elementary and middle school classes. *Science Experiments by the Hundreds* by Cothron, Giese, and Rezba (1996) is an excellent source that will provide you everything needed, including ideas, for conducting experiments. This handbook is used in elementary teacher education programs to provide hands-on ideas about conducting refining and analyzing experiments, finding project ideas, brainstorming project ideas, writing procedures,

experimenting safely, recording data, constructing bar and line graphs, writing an experimental report, conducting interviews, and presenting your experiment. After reviewing the book, you may want to design experiments that are interdisciplinary with science and writing standards.

Stand and Deliver

We live in dynamic times. Teachers must be intellectually dynamic, and they must help students realize a similar dynamism. You are challenged to stand and deliver, an exercise in critical thinking. Reflect on, discuss, weigh, and consider the event. Then, using the key concepts of the chapter, address the questions posed after the scenario.

This scenario raises a difficult issue: cultural change. Should teachers go against family practices and values, as in this incident?

A Time and Place for Everything

Sally Monroe is an eighth-grade math teacher. She takes justifiable pride in her ability to motivate her students. She uses a contract system. The more a student does, the higher his or her grade will be. To earn an A, B, or C, a student must do some homework.

In spite of having done well in sixth-grade math, Frankie Valdez always receives a D—no homework. Mrs. Monroe has written several notes home, explaining that Frankie is a bright student capable of higher achievement, but they have made no difference. One day, Mrs. Monroe runs into Frankie's mother in the grocery store.

"Hello, Mrs. Valdez," she says. "How nice to see you. I must tell you that Frankie is a delight to have in class. He never fools around, and he is always very respectful. When I give him an assignment, he makes sure it is done correctly."

Mrs. Valdez responds, "We have taught him to respect his teachers. He will not give you any trouble."

"Did he show you the notes I sent home?"

"Oh, yes. We read them."

"Frankie has such a high aptitude in math," Mrs. Monroe notes, "but he only does the minimum to get by. Is he a lazy boy at home?"

"Not at all. In fact, he's very good at fixing things around the house."

"Then, why doesn't he do homework?"

Mrs. Valdez pauses, then says, "It is wrong that you give homework. There is a time and place for everything. My husband works hard, and so do I. We don't fool around at work. The day is for work, and the night is for rest and doing what needs to be done at home."

"But don't you want Frankie to be successful? To get a good job? He could do very well with his math skills."

"There's nothing wrong with what my husband and I do for a living—and we believe our family life is as important as what the school may do."

Questions

1. Does Mrs. Monroe's approach foster Frankie's intellectual effectiveness? Why or why not?

2. Does Mrs. Valdez's attitude toward school foster Frankie's intellectual effectiveness?

3. Does Mrs. Valdez's attitude toward school foster or hinder cross-cultural interactions for Frankie?

4. What is wrong in the scenario? What is right? How could you make it better?

nine

Developing Curricula for Diversity

L et us take up curricula that reflect diversity. The previous chapter explains broad-based strategies, but not the method for organizing specific content. Ideally, diverse materials, experiences, and activities permeate the teacher's entire curriculum to assist students in learning about the self and the other. This chapter describes the following steps for building a unique curriculum rich with diverse experiences and activities:

- ❑ Understanding how knowledge is constructed
- ❑ Teaching about culture
- ❑ Using ethnic studies
- ❑ Selecting curriculum materials
- ❑ Fostering student-created curricula
- ❑ Involving parents and others in the curriculum

First, let's define what is meant by *curriculum*.

What Is a Curriculum?

A classroom is defined by teacher and student interactions. The qualities of these interactions are forged by the teacher's academic leadership through a program of study (defined by state and school district curriculum guides) to which he or she has given a unique and personal twist. The unique touch is the teacher—what he or she teaches beyond academic standards and curriculum guides.

Curriculum refers to a course of study teachers and students follow. I resist both the holistic definition (the curriculum is what is taught) as too general and the codified definition (the curriculum is what school authorities mandate to be taught) as too restrictive. Between these extremes is a true middle ground, the stuff teachers develop and the activities they plan inside and outside the mandated subjects.

In most schools, teachers are mandated to follow established curriculum guides and achievement standards. In some instances, the curriculum guides are very broad, providing much more room for a teacher to judge what and how to teach. In other instances, the guides are very specific, allowing little discretion. Usually the guides allow teachers to add unique twists and turns to the course of study.

Grade levels and subject matter also have mandated achievement standards. Whereas curriculum guides outline what should be taught as topics, achievement standards specify academic outcomes in terms of what the students should know or be able to do at a grade level or with a certain subject matter. These achievement standards are used to assess student progress for purposes of accountability.

An entire book could be written about the advantages and disadvantages of standardized achievement standards. Proponents laud standards on the grounds that they force teachers and schools to achieve specific, measurable outcomes rather than allowing for promotion even when students do not meet the standards. Critics argue that standards cause teachers to "teach to the test." Seemingly tangential learning is often ignored in the haste to ensure the students pass the test.

Both views have merit, and a middle ground is emerging. In the meantime, teachers must work with the standards. They are easy to find on the Internet; the education department for each state posts them so they are available to schools statewide. For example, here in Nebraska I need only Google "Nebraska Education Department" to find an array of resources offered by the department at the site www.education.ne.gov, including standards. Later in the chapter, I will demonstrate how cultural lessons can be aligned with state standards.

How do you start a unique curriculum within mandated subjects and standards? It's an age-old challenge. Let's examine one teacher's experience. In *We Fed Them Cactus*, Fabiola Cabeza de Baca wrote:

We opened the morning and afternoon sessions by singing and the children loved it. The Spanish children knew folk songs and the Anglos, cowboy ballads and hillbilly songs. As a reward for good lessons, we sang these, but I also taught them the songs, which are sung in school nowadays. The Star-Spangled Banner resounded on the Mesa Rica each school morning. (1954, p. 56)

A hundred years ago, Fabiola Cabeza de Baca commenced her teaching career in a one-room school in the northeastern *llanos* (plains) of New Mexico. She was painfully aware of her limitations. Although her background in Spanish was strong, she knew little about the backgrounds of either the Anglo or the Native American children.

She learned about her students by boarding in their homes, something not done today. She also was painfully aware of the limitations of her curricular materials. The state-approved American history book—the same book used in Illinois at the time—focused on colonial America and was limited to New England. And even that history was sketchy; it did not mention the French or English presence in nearby Canada, for example. It used only one sentence to include Native Americans— that they helped the pilgrims celebrate Thanksgiving, a Eurocentric myth—and gave another one-sentence nod to the Spanish presence in the faraway Southwest; Southwestern Native Americans weren't mentioned at all.

Undaunted by these limitations, Cabeza de Baca developed her own curriculum in order to equip her students to live in the 20th century. A century later, teachers in modern schools are facing a similar situation. They must, in many cases, devise their own curriculum materials to reflect the diversity that must be recognized in order to live and work in the 21st century.

Let's begin by reviewing how students construct knowledge so that it is meaningful to them.

Understanding How Knowledge Is Constructed

Humans learn by doing and then interpreting what they have done. In the classroom, students learn via experiences with the teacher and others, forming a spiraling vortex of experience (fig. 9.1, page 142).

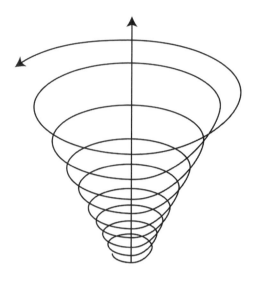

Experience

Figure 9.1: Vortex of experience.

Sources of knowledge surround all students and are rooted in their experiences. People, events, and physical surroundings inform individuals and help them make sense of the seemingly chaotic experiences from which they construct knowledge in an ever-expanding learning spiral. The spiral grows as individuals gain and interpret experiences. This is an ongoing process. Individuals create a personal worldview, an existential construct that integrates experiences with people, events, and emotions into the deepening and expanding spiral, which becomes a coherent window to interpret the world of experiences.

We experience the world around us and learn from it. In *The Children Are Watching: How the Media Teach About Diversity*, Carlos Cortés (2000) describes how the world at large serves as a curriculum to inform children. He calls it a "societal curriculum" by which children develop a worldview that incorporates values and beliefs, perceptions about other people, and observations into their schema. The societal curriculum is broadbased and continual, an informal curriculum (rather than planned) consisting of families, peer groups, neighborhoods, churches, organizations, institutions, mass media, and other forces that educate all of us throughout our lives (Cortés, 2000).

Using the vortex of experience described previously, I believe a child's worldview begins with a focus: first on mother, then on father and other close family, and then on the child's immediate surroundings. Gradually, as the toddler grows, the outdoor world and playmates enter the child's worldview. The child adjusts to the new input by incorporating it into the worldview. The spiral continues upward and outward.

As time passes, the child moves from a relatively small community to the wider influences and inputs of school and other organizations and institutions that involve young people, such as youth groups, sports, clubs, civic groups, church societies, and volunteering.

Childhood today is very different from years past, and a child's worldview is broadened by diverse input early on, mainly because of advanced means of communication and transportation. Children today are exposed to much more at an early age. In Cabeza de Baca's day, students might have had little knowledge beyond their family and the small rural community in which they lived. There were no landline telephones, much less cell phones and the Internet. Automobiles were barely beginning. Air travel had yet to be invented.

The 21st century world comes into the home almost unbidden. Televisions bombard children daily. What I call the "media curriculum" is omnipresent and unavoidable through the Internet, telephones, newspapers, radios, and magazines, all readily available to children. Twenty-first century communication and transportation have ensured that the world and the worldviews of modern children are considerably broader and more diverse than those in Cabeza de Baca's schoolroom. The challenge for educators facing the 21st century is to help their students make sense of a greatly enlarged world.

Much of the development of an individual worldview—or an individual schema—takes place in social contexts, such as the family, community, church, or school. Individual worldviews are embedded within cultures, too: group interaction also creates and perpetuates collective memories, customs, traditions, legends, folkways, and histories.

When children and adolescents come to school, they bring their cultures—a unique potpourri of experiences. The teacher's unique curriculum strives to match those experiences and builds toward new experiences.

Teaching About Culture

Students bob in a cultural stream that flows into the classroom buoyed by a wealth of experiences educators can connect to the school's established curriculum. The student's cultural experiences are embedded in the collective memories of their families and friends. Educators may not be able to learn every language and culture that appears in the classroom, but awareness of and lessons about different cultures are possible.

The crucial term is *about*. Teachers can teach about cultures by linking them to the student's experiences and culture. This is prior knowledge educators can use to scaffold toward new knowledge. Here are suggestions and examples for teaching about culture:

- Seeing the self and the other—Students should learn about the self and the other. In the curriculum, students should experience people and events both inside and outside what they are familiar with. For example, in a children's literature unit, Mexican American students could read books involving Mexican American families, such as Pérez's *My Very Own Room* (2000), about a Mexican American girl who seeks her family's help to make her a bedroom in a very crowded house. After discussing the book, the students could read stories involving families from other cultures, such as Brenner's *Wagon Wheels* (1978) about a freed slave, his sons, and the community of Nicodemus, Kansas—one of the first Great Plains homestead communities formed by freed slaves after the Civil War. While the father is seeking an ideal place to farm, his three brave sons are left to fend for themselves in Nicodemus with other families on the prairie. This comparative approach sends many powerful messages to the Mexican American students. Their culture and other cultures are affirmed.

- Seeing intergroup similarities and differences—Students should examine similarities and differences between cultural groups, as in *My Very Own Room* and *Wagon Wheels*. They should discuss how the families are the same (they are struggling to make the most of their living conditions; all family members contribute in the struggle; both families moved to a new location to seek opportunities), and then discuss how the families differ (ethnic group membership, place, time period). Understanding cross-cultural similarities and differences can be another way to overcome stereotypes and prejudices, engender empathy toward others, and foster a sense of the totality of humanity.

❑ Seeing intragroup diversity—Students should examine the diversity within a cultural group; many variations occur within a culture, and curricular materials should portray this factor. For example, the memoirs *Choteau Creek* (1992) by Yankton Sioux Joseph Iron Eye Dudley and *No Turning Back* (1964) by Hopi Polingaysi Qoyawayma offer an insider's perspective about growing up Native American on the Yankton Sioux and Hopi reservations, respectively. Yet remember that such a viewpoint is personal as well as cultural. Dudley cannot speak for all Yankton Sioux, and Qoyawayma cannot speak for all Hopi. Both describe home and village conditions, but both have very different perspectives shaped by different locations, times, and individual personalities. Qoyawayma speaks of her childhood in an Arizona Indian pueblo during the 1930s and 1940s. Dudley speaks of his childhood on a South Dakota reservation in the 1960s.

These memoirs provide a look into the culture of the two writers. As students analyze the various viewpoints in the memoirs, they will find threads of commonality and differences in cultural values and beliefs among Native Americans. Although students should learn about the common features of a culture, they should also study its variations. It may be worthwhile to speak of groups as a unified whole—the Native American experience—though such descriptions are rarely entirely true. Curricular materials need to clarify such intragroup diversity to dispel misleading images—in short, to characterize, rather than caricature.

❑ Seeing cultures in context—Students should examine a culture within the context of the subjects of the standard curriculum. For example, in most science curriculums, plants are subjects studied at some point in every grade. There is nothing more ordinary than plants, at first glance. In the Great Plains, corn and wheat are common plants. But they are not indigenous. In fact, different people brought them to the Great Plains from different places at different times. Corn was domesticated and cultivated in Mexico more than five thousand years ago. Over the centuries, corn migrated with people, both south and north. In the 19th century, German immigrants brought hardy breeds of wheat from Russia that could withstand frigid winters. They developed what is called "winter wheat," because it can lie fallow beneath the snow. With people and their cultures came the plants. Teachers should browse magazine stands in bookstores or libraries, as these are excellent sources for curriculum material. In most states, the Department of Natural Resources (Game and Fish) publishes interesting and accurate science information.

Consider the following commercially produced science learning kit that examines African cultures within the context of the standard curriculum. The unit is keyed to national science and social studies standards as well as Nebraska's state standards. The specific unit is "African Plant Explorer," from the *Wonderwise: Women in Science Learning Series* video and lesson series (University of Nebraska State Museum & Nebraska 4-H Youth Development, 2001). It contains hands-on activities designed for eight- to twelve-year-olds, keyed to specific grade levels. The Wonderwise website states:

> Dr. Fatimah Jackson is an African American biologist and anthropologist. She studies common African plants that have remarkable uses as food and medicine. Her work takes her to many African countries and to local foods such as cassava, which guards against outbreaks of malaria. She takes samples of these foods back to the lab and investigates their chemical makeup to learn how they work their magic.

In the video, the students are taken to different parts of Africa and introduced to Africa's biodiversity and cultural diversity, as a science lesson. By the time students finish the kit's lessons, they have explored the entire continent, learning that Africa is vast, with more than three thousand ethnic groups who speak over a thousand different languages. This kit suggests many higher-level research topics regarding the migration of plants with simultaneous migration of people and their cultures.

Following are four of the lessons with corresponding Nebraska science and social studies standards (see the interactive links at: http://wonderwise.unl.edu/14africa/afrstandards.htm):

> Activity One—Everyday poisons. Watch a video about scientist Fatimah Jackson and then discover the poisons in everyday foods. Science Standard: Knows that people of all ages, backgrounds, and groups have made contributions to science and technology throughout history.
>
> Activity Two—Investigating Starch. Examine the chemical properties of starch. Science Standard(s): Plans and conducts simple investigations making systematic observations and conducting simple experiments to answer questions. Knows that each plant or animal has different structures, which serve functions in growth, survival, and reproduction.
>
> Activity Three—African Arts. Use cassava to batik African symbols onto cloth. Science Standard: See first standard above. This also fits a Social Studies standard.
>
> Activity Four—Green Travelers. Using maps and videos, explore the world travels of everyday foods. Science and Social Studies Standards: This fits a number of science and social studies standards focused on both physical and cultural geography.

Students should be encouraged to take pride in their cultural heritage and to share it with others as they also learn about different cultures. (Caution: never single out a student to speak as a representative of his or her ethnic or gender group, as in, "Let's hear from Ricardo—he's Mexican American. What do Latinos think about current immigration issues?" Students are individuals with unique perspectives and experiences. We should not assume they are spokespersons for their cultural group.)

Sources of knowledge are all around students. When teachers help students bring their cultures into the classroom, they enrich the classroom environment for all students. In addition, students enhance their own understandings (through introspection) and enlarge their teachers' and their peers' knowledge of their cultures. Students should formalize, create, and select materials to support and extend learning about their cultures and to develop literacy skills, such as presenting reports, developing a sense of voice and audience, and experiencing the power of language (Mélendez & Beck, 2010). Solid facilitative teaching builds on the student's experiences and scaffolds those experiences to higher levels of learning.

Grady (2002) describes a high school in Roseville, Indiana, that incorporated Latino culture throughout its curriculum in response to an influx of mostly Mexican immigrants. The Mexican students were fond of the artwork depicted in a popular magazine, *Lowrider Arte*. They wore T-shirts and carried backpacks emblazoned with it. Grady studied the artwork and found it to be rich with iconography representing various pre-Colombian motifs, early Christian themes such as the Lady of Guadalupe, and ideals from the Mexican Revolution. The art teacher incorporated the magazine's artwork in classes, as a genre of pop art; students were allowed to display their original *Lowrider* drawings and paintings in designated areas. The *Lowrider* project is an example of student-generated materials incorporated in classroom instruction as an integral part of the curriculum, providing literacy activities and critical-thinking exercises that enable students to be responsible for their learning.

Using Ethnic Studies

Another way to teach about a culture is to focus on a specific group in a series of units. This approach falls under the rubric of ethnic studies conceptualized by the scholar James Banks, internationally recognized for scholarship in multicultural studies (Banks, 1973). His book *Teaching Ethnic Studies* provided educators conceptual frameworks for studying about ethnic groups, and while some of its information is dated, the conceptual frameworks are still helpful for teaching about a culture. I organized an ethnic studies model, as follows:

- *Goal*—To foster increased knowledge and understanding of a cultural group

- *Operational assumption*—Increased cultural knowledge will lead to better understanding and acceptance or tolerance of the group studied. (This is the education thesis of reducing prejudice explored in chapter 5.)

❏ *Conceptual frame*—Study is based on the principles that any culture has:

- A dynamic nature

- A system of values and beliefs

- Intragroup diversity; that is, it is internally diverse

- Intergroup similarity; that is, it is both similar to and different from other cultural groups

Ethnic studies may be tailored by a disciplinary focus. For example, rather than investigating all aspects of a cultural group, students in a writing class might focus on literature from the culture under study, or students in a history class might focus on one culture's interactions with another culture over the course of time. Let's examine the principles of the conceptual frame.

A Dynamic Nature

Living cultures are ever changing. Cross-pollination of cultures occurs through contacts that may be made in person or through some form of communication, such as reading books, and results in changing ideas, customs, and products. Twentieth-century transportation and communication advances have made cross-cultural contacts more frequent and more extensive.

Curricular materials need to portray this factor. Too often students are exposed only to a snapshot of a culture, and it may be a stereotypical view at that. For example, when elementary textbooks include information on foreign cultures, they often portray traditional folkways and traditional dress. Students gain a misimpression that such things are the norm when, in fact, traditional dress may be worn only on ceremonial occasions. If culture is reduced to snapshots, then there must be many such snapshots that show a more complete picture of the culture and how it is changing over time.

An example of cultural dynamics is the introduction of the rodeo to the American West (García, 2011). When Anglo cowboys first came into contact with Mexican cowboys in the early 1800s, they noticed the Mexican cowboys played games while waiting for the roundup of stragglers. These were games with such stunts as calf roping and bronco riding, which they carried on during the roundup, or in Spanish, *rodear*. The Anglo cowboys joined in the fun, calling the activities by their version of *rodear*. They pronounced *rodear* as "rodeo." Over time, rodeos became a regular fixture of the Western cattle drive. Eventually, rodeos were organized into the sport that still occurs today—separate from the roundup.

Thus the American cowboy culture was changed by contact with the Mexican cowboy culture.

A System of Values and Beliefs

Curricular materials should portray a culture's basic values and the beliefs that undergird them. Cultural practices have bases in beliefs and values. Conflicting cultural values and beliefs often give rise to prejudice and persecution. Thus gaining an understanding of other cultures can be a first step in combating the destructiveness of cultural prejudices. If students are to understand a culture well, they should examine the culture's practices, traditions, customs, and values.

For example, students might examine the beliefs that support the Japanese value of group identity. The teacher can juxtapose those beliefs against the American beliefs that undergird the value of the individual. The class could pursue this topic through a study of short stories from both countries, by looking at each nation's economic policies and practices, or by probing the historical events leading up to World War II as carried on in the Pacific. Such examination of cultural values and beliefs can be tied to a number of different subjects or disciplines.

Intragroup Diversity

Curricular materials should go beyond the monolithic. Stereotypes portray all individuals within a culture as alike. This is never the reality. No matter how cohesive the group, however commonly held their beliefs, every group is composed of individuals.

Failure to recognize intragroup diversity is endemic to snapshot curricula. Although students need opportunities to learn about the common features of a culture, they should also study the variations. "During the early 1800s, African Americans came to America as slaves" is a snapshot example. Yes, the statement is somewhat true. But others were born in the United States of freed slaves. Absolutes are seldom accurate.

While it may be politically expedient to speak of groups as mono-liths—the Jewish experience, the African American perspective, the Latino position—such descriptions are rarely entirely true. There is great diversity among the experiences of Jews; African Americans hold many viewpoints; and attitudes among Hispanic individuals are as divergent as among the general population. Currently much is made of Islamic culture, as though it were a single entity. In fact, multiple ethnic and national groups adhere to the religion of Islam, reside on every continent, and vary widely in terms of languages, traditions, customs, music, art, and dress.

Good curriculum materials can go far to dispel stereotypes about cultural groups and to reveal the diversity within cultural groups—in short, to characterize, rather than caricature.

Intergroup Similarity

Intergroup similarity is the counterpart of intragroup diversity. Curricular materials need to examine similarities among cultural groups rather than only differences. Too often information provided to students only points out how "the other" is different from them. In fact, many cultural groups have similar beliefs, values, customs, stories, and practices. For example, Islam, Judaism, and Christianity all worship the god of Abraham.

Understanding cross-cultural similarities can be another way to overcome stereotypes and prejudices. Humans tend to demonize those whom they see as different. Therefore, to engender a sense of the totality of humanity, it is important for students to see those from other cultures as like themselves.

Selecting Curriculum Materials

Teachers should select materials that are developmentally appropriate for students' abilities and maturity levels. Nowadays there are tomes of available curriculum materials. Selecting what works best takes careful scrutiny. Some are excellent; others are not. One of my student teachers used a commercially produced lesson on the Mexican custom of celebrating *El Dia de los Muertos* (the Day of the Dead). The lesson inaccurately stated the custom was similar to the American Halloween tradition of masquerading, partying, and trick-or-treating. It is not surprising that people sometimes confuse the Mexican holiday with the American Halloween.

When she realized the inaccuracy, my student exclaimed, "Why, the same lesson was used by my elementary school teacher!" The example makes an important point. Students may remember—or misremember—a lesson many years after it is taught. Selection and presentation of accurate materials are crucial. Teaching is a scholarly pursuit; there is no substitute for accurate knowledge. Here are questions to consider when selecting curricular materials to teach about culture:

- What is your purpose for selecting the materials? How will the materials allow you to expand upon the mandated curriculum? This is about enrichment. Most curriculum guides describe broad categories or topics to be covered. Selected materials should expand upon the established curriculum or go beyond it. The teacher's job is to uncover as much as possible, infusing diverse information and activities into the lessons.

- For what purpose were the materials developed? This is about pertinence. The authors should state the intended purpose for the materials. Does their purpose match yours? You may have to adapt the materials to fit grade levels, reading abilities, or other developmental factors.

- What are the qualifications of the authors of the materials? This is about accuracy. Are the writers of the materials authorities on the subject? How is that expertise shown? Do they have professional credentials or direct experience with the topic? Have they written books, journal articles, or conducted research on the topic?

- What sources did the authors use to write the materials? This criterion is also about accuracy; how do the authors support opinions? Is the support plausible? What sources are cited? Selecting accurate materials takes caution but need not be daunting. Remember that cultures are dynamic and diverse, and people hold multiple perspectives about them. When presenting the materials, tell the students where you found the information and why you think it is correct, noting that knowledge changes as new information is discovered.

Finding curriculum materials and ideas to teach should be an ongoing project. It's okay to take ideas from others, just give credit. For example, Larkin and Sleeter (1995) organize multicultural lessons within most school subjects at both elementary and secondary levels. Manning and Baruth (2009) suggest lessons for most U.S. ethnic minority groups. In addition, they provide lessons about Arab Americans and European American children and adolescents.

I keep a file, actually many files, called "found lessons." The textbooks mentioned previously are among the many sources for ideas. There is nothing wrong with borrowing ideas for lessons from others. Give them credit for the idea in some way, but make their idea your own by tweaking it to fit you and your intentions for the lesson. As you work to make your curriculum materials and activities unique, think of these summary guidelines:

- Treat cultural expressions with respect—Avoid cultural elitism, such as labeling one expression "high culture" and another "low culture." Such elitism also extends to judgments about validity, such as characterizing a single-parent home as a "broken home." Two-parent homes can be broken or dysfunctional, and single-parent homes can be healthy and vital.

- Celebrate cultures in context—The "heroes and holidays" approach is limited; digging deeper into cultures reveals a richer reality. That said, cultural holidays and events should still be celebrated. For example, it is appropriate to celebrate the memory of Martin Luther King Jr. on the memorial holiday in January, but it is inappropriate to then ignore African American issues and culture the rest of the year.

- Consider your students as good sources for ideas—This allows students to bring their cultures into the classroom. Try to engage them in the development of lessons through researching, cooperative learning, and interviewing. (More on this topic later.)

❏ Try for breadth and depth—Too narrow a focus can exclude diversity. For example, in teaching a unit on World War II, one curricular focus might be the strategies used by the winning generals. While this approach will provide one perspective on how the Allies succeeded in winning the war, it also will neglect much of the real work of the soldiers under those generals, such as units of African Americans, Japanese, Native Americans, and women whose work both in and out of uniform was an essential element of the Allied success. My point is that World War II is an enormous topic. It is legitimate to narrow the topic, but in so narrowing, it also is important to ensure that the topic remains broad enough to admit diversity.

Fostering Student-Created Curricula

Students' cultural experiences manifest as stories, traditions, special vocabulary, and even recipes. These memories are the stuff of student-created curriculum materials. Student-generated curricula have a powerful immediacy and relevance. I began this chapter with a quote from Fabiola Cabeza de Baca's book, the spirit of which bears reiteration—students should be encouraged to bring their cultures to school. The older melting pot view cajoled students to leave their cultures outside the schoolhouse door and embrace a new culture within; however, teaching for diversity means encouraging students to do the opposite. By bringing their cultures into the classroom, students can enhance their own understandings (through introspection) and enlarge their teachers' and peers' knowledge of their cultures.

When teachers help students formalize a curriculum and create or select curricular materials to support and extend learning, they also are teaching important skills. For example, they can help students develop a sense of voice and audience as well as understand the power of language. When students see and hear others responding to their curriculum materials, they realize that they can influence how others create knowledge and build understanding.

The making of curricula need not be confined to older students. Younger students have written and illustrated books for a long time. For example, in 1976, a friend of mine, Chon La Brier, principal of the Dulce Public Schools on the Jicarilla Apache Reservation in New Mexico, gave me books written and illustrated by the third-grade pupils of Teresa Casaus and Gloria Brinks. Titled *My Name is . . .*, *I Am Me*, and *All About Me*, the book covers feature smiley faces, and inside are words and drawings by and about the pupil. Topics in the books cover biographic details such as where and when the student was born, likes and dislikes, and recreational activities and home chores.

Each year the students created books, and each year more students read and discussed the books within the school's established curriculum, in which reading and writing were simultaneously taught and learned. This is solid constructivist teaching, building on the student's experiences and scaffolding that experience to younger pupils.

Kathryn Au (1993) describes several student-developed curricula that involve very young students. Kindergartners in a Seattle school planned and created a ten-minute video and six small books to show younger children what it would be like to enter kindergarten. The materials covered such topics as the school bus, recess, and lunch, and sought to quell fears that newcomers might have about coming to kindergarten. The kindergartners were explaining the school culture to those who would follow them into it.

Student-generated curricula are now a time-honored practice. Other examples of curricula and materials that even quite young students can develop include:

- Research projects and reports
- Panel discussions, debates, and forums
- Articles for school and local newspapers
- Stories for telling and reading, skits, and scripts
- Family stories, customs, recipes, and genealogies
- Electronic or computer-generated visuals
- Visual displays, dioramas, and bulletin boards

The research needed to create a curriculum is the key for students at any level, and can be modified for grade level. Students analyze cultural information, taking a proactive approach to gathering such information rather than receiving it passively. They bring together diverse information and construct new knowledge by adding to and modifying their prior understandings. And they evaluate knowledge, deciding what is most worth knowing and determining actions based on such evaluation.

Research is not only for advanced classes or grades. Kindergarteners can conduct research, as in the Au (1993) example, adapted for their experiential level and maturity. Students may pose research questions on their own, or teachers can ask the students to pose problems. (See chapter 8 on critical thinking.) They will need guidance, but they are curious about a lot of things. The students can conduct research on the problem via family stories, family or community interviews, and library and Internet searches. Teachers should facilitate the research activities by providing guidance on how to:

- Collect and write family stories
- Ask good questions in an interview
- Access and assess library and Internet sources
- Write a research report
- Recount the results of the report, either orally or in writing, such as a class report or a letter to the editor

Treat research as a voyage of discovery, because that's what it is—a trip from a known port into uncharted waters in which students can take responsibility for their learning. Through research based on critical thinking, students can be best prepared to debunk stereotypes and combat biases regarding race, socioeconomic status, ethnicity, gender, sexual orientation, and the like. They will experience the power of knowledge and how it can be used. This is no trivial experience.

Student-generated curriculum materials represent the best of teaching. They are authentic, original creations that provide students a venue to find and express their voices. They are inherently empowering, and when used in conjunction with classroom activities, they inspire students to become active initiators of their own learning.

Involving Parents and Others in the Curriculum

Students' parents and others from the community are equally valuable in these classroom activities. Teaching is a shared responsibility between teachers and parents, yet parents and others in the local community are often overlooked as a source for curriculum activities and materials. Conscientious teachers may feel reluctant or burdened because they feel responsible for providing all the information in the curriculum, or they may be reluctant to ask for assistance because parents and community members have busy schedules, or in some instances, have had a bad experience with schools when they were children. Forget those concerns. Most adults are pleased to be asked because an invitation is acknowledgment they have something important to contribute to the education of children.

The parents of every student are a potential resource. Their special talents will become apparent if they are involved in the classroom. Keep parents involved by engaging them in the development of student-created curriculum materials and by sending home examples of their children's work with your comments attached. Emphasize the positive. When sending home notes, make sure they are translated, if needed, for parents who may not know English. You may have to identify someone in the community to translate for you, although larger school districts often hire bilingual home-school liaisons.

Learn parents' names, and make sure you pronounce them correctly. Work with the students or parents to teach you how to pronounce the names, spelling them out phonetically so you can practice. This simple act will achieve volumes in trust and rapport. If the parents are able to assist as guest speakers, they may be able to identify others in the community. Keep a file with names, full contact information, telephone numbers, email addresses, and so on. Ask fellow teachers, the principal, and others in central administration for necessary information. Again, home-school liaisons can be of immense help.

Parental involvement need not be onerous. Simply encourage parents to pay attention to their child's homework. Have the child explain the homework, what must be done, and after it's done, what does it look like. Parents can ask questions and offer praise. Also, remind parents, their child will emulate them. If the child sees parents reading, they too will read, if reading materials are available.

When you invite parents or other community members to your class, link them to your curriculum. Before they come to school, explain how the presentation or activity will connect to what students are learning. This is important. The guests are there to be more than an entertaining diversion; they are enriching the curriculum. If not, they will detect it. When the guests arrive at school, have them check in at the principal's office, where one or more students can greet and escort them to class. When they are finished, make sure to give thanks with a token of appreciation, a follow-up thank you note, or materials produced by students.

Finally, do not overlook your community as a curriculum resource. Much can be taught in most subjects via the community's physical and cultural geography, churches, cemeteries, plants and factories, farms, and so on. Outside the school, local city, county, and state offices, libraries, and local churches may be of assistance. The U.S. Department of Agriculture's Cooperative Extension System is a non-credit educational network. Each U.S. state and territory has a state office at its land-grant university and a network of local or regional offices with one or more experts who provide useful, practical, and research-based information to agricultural producers, small business owners, youth, consumers, *schools*, and others in rural areas and communities of all sizes, even metropolitan areas.

Remember Veronica Martinez and Colfax, Nebraska, from chapter 1? The community started as a one-industry town: family farming. Today it is still a one-industry town, but now the industry is meatpacking. The first citizens were Germans; now they are Latinos. Colfax is rich in history for all kinds of lessons in science (farming and meatpacking) and cultural geography (German refugees from Russia, Latinos from Mexico and Honduras). Sources for curriculum are everywhere; the world is a teacher's classroom. In practical terms, the local community—its students, parents, members, and physical and cultural geography—make vital, relevant sources.

Obviously, I favor curricula generated by teachers, their pupils, parents, and others in the community, such as using family histories for reading or for panel discussions in middle and high school social studies. These are critical thinking exercises that enable students to be responsible for their learning. But even when teachers are mandated to teach from a standardized curriculum, nothing prevents them from infusing it with materials they have developed within the local community. The multitude of print and nonprint resources available can be adapted to suit local classrooms and students.

Fabiola Cabeza de Baca was on the right track when she encouraged her Spanish- and English-speaking children to bring their cultures to school in songs and stories. Yet she had few resources compared to teachers nowadays. Undaunted, she developed her own curriculum materials. In our time, there is no excuse for excluding teacher- and student-generated curricula. Students should be encouraged to take pride in their cultural heritage and to share that pride and knowledge with others, just as they learn about different cultures. Sources of knowledge are all around them. When teachers help and encourage students to bring their cultures into the classroom, they enrich the environment for all students and make teaching for diversity a reality.

Reflections

1. Develop a unique cultural curriculum using the ethnic studies approach. Focus on one group to develop the materials and activities to teach about that group, following the ethnic studies matrix described in this chapter.

2. Develop a lesson that uses student-created curriculum materials. Specify what the materials will look like when done. Make sure the materials are linked to skills or topics mandated by a school district's guides.

3. In teams with colleagues, role-play the following situations, and then discuss them:

   a. Encountering and placating an angry parent

   b. Encouraging reluctant parents to get involved in their children's education

   c. Providing tips to parents to assist with their children's homework

4. Read and discuss the following Stand and Deliver scenario. Follow up with the challenge activity posed.

Stand and Deliver

We live in dynamic times. Teachers must be intellectually dynamic, and they must help students realize a similar dynamism. You are challenged to stand and deliver, an exercise in critical thinking. Reflect on, discuss, weigh, and consider the event. Then, using the key concepts of the chapter, address the questions posed after the scenario.

Myth or Truth?

Ninth-grade teacher Bob Jones was teaching literature approved in the school district's curriculum as an extension of what the students had already read: Greek, Roman, and Norse myths. During a unit on ethnic literature, Mr. Jones introduced the topic of the creation of the world, as described by various cultures. First, the class read and studied the Old Testament's Genesis from the King James Bible. They then studied the poem by James Weldon Johnson, "The Creation," which describes the account from Genesis.

Next, Mr. Jones assigned a reading about a Native American story about the creation of the Onondaga, a Northeast Woodlands tribe (Bruchac, 1991). Following is a summarized version of the tale he assigned:

> Ancient Chief lived above the sky with his wife. One day the wife fell through a hole in the sky. An eagle caught her and placed her on the back of a large turtle. Other turtles gathered mud from the ocean bottom. Soon a great island existed. The eagle brought grass and twigs from far away. They grew. Ancient Chief asked his wife to return. She refused and said she wanted to stay on the ground where all kinds of plants had grown. Ancient Chief granted her wish. Then she had a son. Soon the whole island was filled with people. That is how the first Indians were created. (Bruchac, 1991)

When parents became aware of the reading, several voiced objections to the assignment. They objected on grounds that:

- ❑ The story taught strange ideas about God, such as he had a wife and allowed the wife to leave him.

- ❑ The first man, the wife's son, was born of a female God.

- ❑ The story raised a question about who the father of the wife's son might be.

Mr. Jones responded that the Onondaga myth left many questions unanswered, as did the creation myth in Genesis. The parents countered angrily that the biblical accounts of creation of the earth, universe, and the first man and woman were truths, not myths.

Author's Comments

Mr. Jones continues to teach ninth-grade literature and has been recognized for his excellence. He was kind enough to share this incident and allow us to learn. According to his assessment, he was right and wrong in this incident.

He was right to go beyond the school's Eurocentric curriculum that only focused on European folklore. He was right to go from the known to the unknown: from the account in Genesis to the Native American account. However, he was wrong to introduce the entire unit on myths and creation stories without involving the parents. Furthermore, he should have informed the parents of the unit's contents and place in the language arts curriculum, allowing the parents to discuss it with him. He was wrong to assume there would be no parental criticism of his approach. The criticism arose because parents did not understand his approach. He should have informed the students and parents via a note sent home about the topic, being careful with terminology, *account* rather than *myth*, for example. Notice that scholars will call an account a myth, which may be technically correct. Unfortunately, to many people, the term *myth* refers to falsehood. Teachers have to be sensitive to the backgrounds of their students and parents.

Your Challenge

Put yourself in the place of Mr. Jones. The critical parents ask you (Mr. Jones) to teach the creation story account taken from a book on creation science. Remember you have already taught creation stories from Europe, the Old Testament, and the Native American story. How will you handle the parents' request? Remember, you are teaching a literature course. The parents are not asking you to teach the story as science. Realize that you are not alone; some schools have department heads or curriculum directors to assist you, and of course, the principal or assistant principal can be involved.

ten

Building Community in Diverse Classrooms

D iversity is a fact of life. Community is not. It must be envisioned, nurtured, and fostered to thrive. Schools are called upon to assist families in rearing children to live well. Bringing up children to live successfully in the greater community has been a shared responsibility for a very long time. More than a hundred years ago, Jane Addams wrote in *Democracy and Social Ethics*:

> The democratic ideal demands of the school that it shall give the child's own experience a social value; that it shall teach him to direct his activities and adjust them to those of other people. (1907, p. 180)

The adage "It takes a village to raise a child" rings true. In fact, schools are like village commons, the place in communal living where individuals pull together for the development of the self in conjunction with others. Each honors the rights of others so that others will honor hers or his. This is an old ideal, a social contract inherent in e pluribus unum.

In prior chapters, I focused on the intellectual development of students via instruction guided by three universal goals: (1) learning autonomy, (2) intellectual effectiveness, and (3) cultural efficacy. I examine those goals again in this chapter through the lens of socialization (social development), which is mainly "caught" rather than taught in daily classroom and school interactions. First, I examine the relationship between socialization and diversity; then I discuss the characteristics fundamental to a community, from which I make inferences for building community in the classroom. I conclude with a discussion of the school as a village commons.

Socialization and Diversity

Socialization within a learning community is the process of teaching and learning social values necessary for living in a free society. It fosters self-respect and respect for the views and rights of others. Take kissing, for example. Travel back to a second-grade class in 1950; during recess, Dick chases Jane in a game of stealing kisses. Dick boasts, "Georgie Porgie, puddin' an' pie, kisses the girls and makes them cry!" Jane runs away, giggling. When Dick catches her, he plants a kiss on her cheek and yells, "Gotcha!" Jane doesn't cry.

Meanwhile, another second-grader, Skipper, wants Johnny to be her boyfriend. After lunchtime play, they are hanging up their coats. Alone in the hallway for a moment, Skipper slips up behind Johnny, spins him around, and quickly kisses his cheek. Johnny objects and later complains to his mother, who complains to the teacher.

In 1950, Dick's unwanted kiss was okay, but Skipper's was not. In that time, cultural values held that boys could kiss anybody they wanted, but girls could not.

Today, a kiss is not just a kiss. Now we wonder, are kisses only child's play? Or is there something more going on—one kiss in conquest, one of unwelcome affection, as shown here, and still another for comforting a hurt like a skinned knee or bruised feelings? In the 21st century, with its headlines about alleged sexual harassment in elementary schools, Dick's and Skipper's unwanted kisses might push some educators to ban all kisses in second grade. That would be a legalistic solution, but not an educational one. In that situation, students may learn it is okay to kiss somebody whenever you want and however you want, as long as you don't get caught. A ban teaches in the negative—don't kiss, or don't get caught. It does not address the ethical or moral reasons for a ban on unwanted kisses.

My point is that teaching social values also means exploring the motivations and reasons behind our actions in various social contexts. A kiss of innocent comfort is different from a kiss in conquest or an unwanted expression of affection. It is those differences that educators must elucidate and students must learn or, in many cases, discover for themselves—hopefully within a supportive environment.

Teaching for diversity treads similarly choppy water. As society grows increasingly diverse, there are few pat generalizations about correct norms for classroom and school behavior. We fall back on core beliefs: equality of opportunity and e pluribus unum. Fused together, the two beliefs form the nexus of a social contract. In schools and classrooms, students are entitled to equal opportunity and are obligated to honor the individual rights of others.

The social contract is so embedded in Western societies that it is often taken for granted, an unconscious promise citizens make and sometimes break. The norms—rules of engagement—of the contract are learned at home and at school from parents, teachers, and community members.

Times change, people change, and the contract's rules change. Dick's 1950 kiss of conquest is seen differently in the light of the 21st century, as is Skipper's kiss. Teachers and parents have to work together to make the norms explicit so children will learn the boundaries for their behavior. If it takes a village, why not simulate a village in the classroom? If students learn how to function well in the microcosmic community of the classroom, then they will be more likely to assume attitudes and behaviors to allow them to function well in the larger human community beyond the schoolyard.

A 21st Century Global Village

A village is the manifestation of a primordial instinct. It is the human impulse to nest, settle, and sustain a place called home. A village is a physical representation of community: an organization of people living and working together in common cause. Some communities are defined by geographic lines, others by less tangible boundaries of language or shared interests. Classrooms too can be communities.

A village's best features suggest the best features of a democratic society. These can be summed up as (1) having a common purpose, (2) maintaining stability, (3) fostering cooperation, and (4) balancing independence and interdependence. Each of these characteristics merits a few words about its application to the classroom community.

Common Purpose

To function as a community, any group must have one or more common purposes. In this context, *purpose* refers to a classroom's raison d'etre, a reason or justification for existence. A similar perspective is that *purpose* refers to an ideal one desires to make real in its application. The overriding ideal or purpose of attending school is to learn—perhaps, more accurately, to learn how to learn. Along with this purpose, school attendance should foster an individual's academic and social development. These purposes are discussed throughout this book as the educational goals of learning autonomy, intellectual effectiveness, and cultural efficacy. More specific purposes complement these basic purposes, such as to learn how to read or how to speak another language.

Keep in mind a classroom community exists within the context of a school, but it also exists within a community context. The school serves the local community, state, national, and even the global community. While a classroom's purposes are explicitly designed for a specific classroom, we should remember a classroom does not exist in a vacuum.

Stability

Historically, villages were stabilized by traditions and established norms. Everybody knew the traditions and rules, although few had any say about them. Today, communities create their own traditions and rules. In the classroom, teachers should provide the leadership to implement simple rules for classroom behavior, while giving students the opportunity to shape or tweak them. The rules should be based on a balance between the rights of the individual and the rights of the class as a whole. In other words, "your rights end where the rights of others begin." Students should treat others with mutual respect.

In some classrooms, the student population is relatively stable, providing teachers an easy setting to establish rules and maintain them. In other classrooms, transiency is an issue, as in schools serving military families and some schools serving low-income families. Students come and go, making it difficult to maintain a set of known rules and procedures. In classrooms of high transiency, it is essential that teachers provide newcomers a way to learn classroom rules and procedures. I have seen a peer system work: the teacher assigns the newcomer a friend in the class whose job is to teach the new student the ropes, explain the classroom rules, and assist the newcomer in any other way.

Cooperation

A village is not merely a collection of individuals all going about their business unaware of one another. In fact, a functional village requires genuine interaction among individuals. Schools and classrooms provide a training ground for building an ideal village—a commons—for students to learn how to pursue individual interests while concurrently respecting the rights of others to pursue their individual interests. Cooperation is the medium for students to learn to balance self-interests and social responsibilities. In other words, proximity does not equate to community. Rather, community means that students respond to one another, work together, help one another, and take on tasks that draw out individual talents for common ends.

Independence and Interdependence

In order to function successfully, Western democracies must balance independence (individualism) with interdependence (collaboration). The watchwords are *freedom within order*. Students need to learn how to work well with one another and how to determine when a task can best be done alone or with others. Critical and creative thinking are essential for a modern community to function, and contemporary communications and information-age commerce necessitate community-building on a global scale.

Canadian cultural critic and communication theorist Marshall McLuhan, with Bruce R. Powers (1989), coined the phrase *global village*. He was thinking of a network of people who are linked electronically. He described the global village as a computer-based satellite and media network. The emergence of computer technology and satellite television has indeed allowed us to link with strangers in a global web of electronic-based relationships. But there is more to the global village notion than electronics; it also includes what electronic connections have permitted. For example, such technology also facilitates and speeds economic links. Globalization of national economies is changing the notion of community, as nations with very different value systems are forced to seek ways to cooperate in order to do business.

Urbanization has also changed the nature of community. Cities are often collections of small villages in the form of ethnic neighborhoods and enclaves built on lines of socioeconomic status, class, language, race, or other factors. Modern communication and transportation, democratic social initiatives such as desegregation, the continuing influx of immigrants, and other forces in the new information age constantly reshape these villages.

Yet some communities remain insular, not out of choice but circumstance. In rural and urban areas without the economic resources to support an electronic network, for example, there exists a digital divide. These areas are not connected well to the global village because they cannot afford the expensive technology needed to interface with others outside their villages. In fact, because of poverty, some children have no access to others beyond their immediate neighborhoods. Here schools can serve an important function—linking students to the broader society.

Building a Classroom Community

In earlier chapters, I suggested that the role of education is to foster viable individuals. Viable individuals are capable of sustaining independent living, which requires getting along with others. A classroom community should provide opportunities for students to learn how viable, conscientious adults balance self-interests with the interests of others.

Such a community of learners begins with the school leaders and teachers who are collectively responsible for providing a safe environment conducive to learning (Madsen & Mabokela, 2005). In chapter 6, I sketched a broad definition of safety that includes emotional and physical safety. Students must feel safe to be themselves and to think for themselves, even when their backgrounds, lifestyles, and ideas diverge from others.

In *Transforming School Culture* (2009), Anthony Muhammad describes the difference between *technical* and *cultural* change. Though his book addresses whole-school change, the ideas can be applied to classrooms as well. Technical changes are changes in tools, such as new textbooks or instructional strategies. These are surface changes effective for the short term. Cultural changes are deeper changes promising long-term effectiveness. They have to do with both attitude and behavior changes in teachers and students.

Within the classroom, the teacher is the leader who sets the tone and direction of the classroom community, a village in which the students will function as interdependent scholars. Together, teacher and students work to balance individual and group concerns. These balancing acts include:

- Building trust among students
- Building trust with parents
- Pursuing self-interests and the common good
- Behaving independently and interdependently
- Practicing individual rights and respecting others

Each of these balancing acts are interrelated and merit further discussion.

Building Trust Among Students

Cooperative learning activities are an excellent way to build trust among students. Briefly, cooperative learning is an approach in which small groups use various learning activities to improve their understanding of subject matter, interact responsibly, and develop social skills through sharing of information, learning objectives, and outcomes. Two established cooperative learning programs, Group Investigation Model (GIM) (Sharan et al., 1984; Thelen, 1954) and Student Achievement Divisions (STAD) (Slavin, 1983) can be used with almost any subject and almost any grade. With GIM, students work cooperatively to produce a group project. Their research and research results reflect the use of higher-order or critical thinking. With STAD, students of different academic ability work together in four- to five-member teams. They study together what the teacher has already taught with the goal of helping each student reach his or her highest level of achievement. Students are then tested individually and teams are recognized in some way based on the team members' progress over their past record.

Students require guidance to work effectively in a team. They need assistance in the development of interpersonal skills, such as keeping an open mind, listening to others, sharing information, and not interrupting each other (Johnson, Johnson, & Holubec, 1988).

Cooperative learning tends to improve academic achievement by having students draw on the strengths of others for learning new information.

Students help one another in the acquisition of information and the construction of meaning through discussion, debate, and negotiation (Johnson & Johnson, 2010). Broad arrays of studies have demonstrated cooperative learning's effectiveness on various outcomes. Some related to themes in this book are: enhanced relations among ethnic groups, increased academic achievement for lower- and middle-income students, and improved mainstreaming of students with learning disabilities (Balkcom, 1992).

Having students work in groups is a common method. To me, cooperative learning takes the method to greater depth and is a very well-designed approach for students to conduct group work. My research on the general characteristics of the cooperative learning method revealed at least four characteristics that distinguish it from ad hoc group work: (1) in a group, individual accountability and positive interdependence operate concurrently; (2) before group work begins, social interaction skills have been described; (3) during group work, the social interaction skills described in the second step are implemented and monitored; and (4) after the group's objectives are completed, group members take the time to assess how effective the group worked together to complete its objectives and discuss ways they might improve the group experience.

From the teacher's standpoint, cooperative learning is an active-learning approach to instruction. Roselle Kline Chartock (2010) demonstrates how teachers can produce culturally responsive classroom communities via cooperative learning techniques. She also provides a prejudice reduction approach via cooperative learning.

Students who are permitted to work with one another cannot sustain a passive role for long, as they might in a teacher-centered classroom. Once the teacher has explained the general procedures of cooperative learning, she then typically assigns students to four- or five-member teams. In most cooperative learning situations the students are mixed by ability (including students with disabilities) and other factors as known, such as race, gender, social class, and so on. This integration of students helps make cooperative learning a powerful strategy in teaching for diversity.

The student teams are provided with, or decide for themselves, how to achieve the instructional objectives. Each member of the cooperative team will be expected to assist in the attainment of the group goals, as well as to achieve his or her individual objectives. Assessment must follow this principle, too. Teachers must evaluate attainment of both group and individual objectives.

As students work on academic subject matter, they must communicate with one another; they must discuss ideas, share information, compromise, and resolve conflicts, all of which must be accomplished with civility, maintaining an acceptable level of classroom decorum. Students also work out differences and develop important social skills. They develop study relationships and friendships across lines of difference.

Part of the power of cooperative learning is its immediacy. Students learn, in part, by teaching one another, which fosters both interdependence and self-reliance. One student cannot always be the teacher; he or she must occasionally take the role of the student, and vice versa. Well-structured cooperative learning situations reduce students' sense of risk. Being wrong simply means that someone will help, someone in the group will know the right answer, and everyone will benefit—and no student will be wrong all the time.

I have painted the rosiest picture of cooperative learning for building trust among students. But, of course, successful collaboration does not just happen. It is learned. And a major part of learning to cooperate— beyond simple sharing and turn-taking—is learning how to resolve conflicts.

Building Trust With Parents

Cooperative learning is an excellent way to build trust among students, but we should not forget parents. Teachers and students should engage parents and other community members in the classroom community. To begin, formalize a class contract, that is, an explicit agreement about the classroom's rules and expected behaviors for all students. It should be written by and for students, when practical, which they take home and discuss with their parents. It should be translated into the home language for parents who aren't comfortable with English, if needed. Parents should be asked for input into the contract as well as signatures to show they have received and understood it. If major issues arise, speak with the parents to assuage concerns and attend to differences.

Use the contract to discuss the student's behavior and academic performance when meeting with parents during the year. Classroom guests, mainly members of the community, should also be informed of the general agreements within the contract so they will know what to expect when making a presentation or just visiting the class.

Pursuing Self-Interests and the Common Good

Pursuing self-interests in addition to the common good is a balancing act between the individual's rights and the rights of others. It is desirable that students are autonomous and self-directed, but other students and the class as a whole have to be considered. For example, suppose Puma, a fifth-grade Native American student, is fascinated by the history of the Sioux, who are important in his heritage. The fifth-grade curriculum requires students to study the opening of the American West, but the standard textbook approaches the subject almost entirely from the white settlers' point of view. How can the teacher and the students balance the requirements of the curriculum with sensitivity to diversity generally and to individual interests, such as Puma's?

One way might be to supplement the textbook with other viewpoints on the opening of the West, including the views of the Sioux during that period. That could answer the general diversity concern. Another strategy might be to allow students to extend their learning about the opening of the West by choosing individual research projects. Puma might choose to do research about the Sioux, and other students would be free to choose other topics related to the general theme. Such curricular adaptations would serve to balance students' individual interests, which often are expressions of self-interest, and the common good, served by the topic or theme of general study.

Certainly, the teacher might structure an instructional approach to the topic along these lines without involving students in such planning, but it is much more valuable for the students when they can take part in devising ways to accommodate diversity and individual interests. By involving students in making such decisions, teachers help students learn not only the subject matter at hand but also how to work together, how to address diversity issues, and how to balance self-interest and the common good.

Behaving Independently and Interdependently

This balancing act is similar to the prior. Free societies operate with a high value placed on independence of the individual. The democracies of Canada and the United States prize self-reliance and individual initiative, but they also must weigh that freedom against the needs of the society as a whole. The freedom of the individual must always be balanced against the good of the community and the nation.

Classroom communities must function as microcosms of the larger community. Students must learn self-reliance and how to take initiative, but they also must learn how to work with others, compromise, and cooperate. For example, suppose four students are expected to work together on an art project, a paper mural to be mounted in the hallway. The teacher might initiate this project by discussing with students how the task could be approached, or mark off four sections on the large paper and let each student work independently. But this strategy would hardly produce a cohesive mural. A better alternative might be to encourage students to talk about their individual strengths.

For example, Matt is very good at drawing human figures. Steve does best with animals, such as horses and dogs. Ellen can handle trees, buildings, and flowers well. And Veronica is very good at drawing vehicles, such as cars and trains. By tapping their individual skills and then pooling their resources, the students can produce a mural with many well-drawn elements. This strategy maintains students' independence while also requiring that they plan and work interdependently.

Cooperation of this type is not without precedent. The astute teacher also might seize this teachable moment to discuss medieval and early Renaissance artists' schools and studios, in which several artisans would work under the guidance of a master to collectively produce works of art. Such collaborative art was once the norm, and it continues although it is less visible in our time. For example, the glass artist Dale Chihuly has not blown glass for several decades, due to an injury in 1979. He designs the glass that bears his name in exhibitions, but others do the actual glass blowing (see the Wikipedia entry on Dale Chihuly for more information: http://en.wikipedia.org/wiki /Dale_Chihuly). My point is that helping students learn how to balance independence with interdependence need not be approached merely as an isolated socialization exercise. Indeed, it would seem artificial to do so. Rather, socialization should take place in the regular context of teaching standard subject matter.

Practicing Individual Rights and Respecting Others

For every right, there is a concurrent responsibility. Another balancing act concerns the rights and responsibilities of individuals and groups. Let's examine a concrete example. Students in a fourth-grade class are required to keep a daily journal. This is an individual responsibility, but it is expected of all students. For example, Eileen writes about what happens in her life. Some of what she writes is personal. When students are invited to share their journal entries, Eileen is embarrassed. How might the teacher and students cooperate to honor Eileen's right to privacy and still fulfill the expectations of the assignment, which is a group responsibility?

One approach might be to allow all students to keep two-part journals: one part labeled "private," the other "public." Eileen can fulfill her individual journal-keeping responsibility and still maintain her right to privacy. When sharing time rolls around, Eileen can feel free—as can other students—to share only the public portion of her journal. At the same time, students might discuss how to honor individual expressions. They should be responsible as a group for their behavior. They might collectively determine a set of guidelines, such as thanking the individual for sharing his or her ideas, asking constructive questions, and responding without judging.

Again, while the teacher might direct students to these ends, the lesson will be learned at a deeper level if students discuss the issues and come to their own decisions under the teacher's guidance.

The Teacher's Learning Community

Building a learning community takes concerted effort, but it is within a teacher's grasp. As a final note, consider that teachers, too, can benefit from working in a community of peers—a professional learning community. A community can be built with peers on site in the same building, with global peers in online communities, or with the world of ideas in educational research. It never hurts to listen to the experience of others. For example, DuFour, Eaker, and DuFour's *On Common Ground* (2008) collects the insights of researchers and practitioners attempting to implement learning communities in their schools. Or you might want to read *The Collaborative Teacher* (Erkens et al., 2008). Here ten practicing teachers compiled an anthology of specific techniques, with supporting research and classroom examples, about how to collaborate with others to build a viable curriculum and make data-based decisions about instruction.

Schools as Village Commons

Teachers can build community in their classrooms, yet they depend on school leaders, principals, and other administrators to build a community spirit in their schools. If the leaders involve teachers in the process, a positive school community is likely.

Schools are the closest places to a town's commons in American communal life. Here children and their families gather to pursue self-interests and the interests of the greater community. Schools reflect the communities from which they draw their students, teachers, and others involved in the education enterprise. These communities are not only the physical surroundings—the farms, houses, apartments, and businesses that serve them—but also the affinity groups: the Hmong community, the Latino community, the deaf community, the gay community, and so on.

Schools are also communities in themselves. Another way of expressing this notion is that schools are an extension of the family and, by extrapolation, are families themselves—as communities are families by extension.

This circular definition points at the fact that communities, families, and schools own many characteristics in common. Not least among these characteristics is that group viability (as school, as family, as community) is firmly tied to individual viability. In a free society, the school must rely—as the community must—on the civil interactions of its participants, who act out of respect for individuals who may be different from themselves and with whose opinions they may not always agree. As siblings in a family may hold divergent viewpoints, so, too, may citizens disagree. However, as effective families stick together in spite of differences, so, too, do communities and schools stick together by using the glue of civility and respect for diversity to achieve social unity.

Social unity permits schools to function as learning communities working toward universal education goals. When the social unity of a school breaks down, then it cannot succeed in fostering individual learning, much less universal education. Breakdowns of social unity may arise from conflicts over diversity issues. Racial prejudice, denigration of a (non-English) native language, homophobia, and other attitudes of intolerance are root causes of social disunity. Intolerance disrupts learning; unchecked, it may destroy learning.

As microcosms of the larger community (whether *larger* is taken to be local or global), schools are also a social preparation for adult community life. Educators must ensure that schools are exemplars of effective community life in a democratic society. In the context of teaching for diversity, the building of effective community requires educators to form partnerships and to solve diversity problems.

Schools function best as exemplars of community when educators form partnerships with their constituents. Those constituents are not only students and their parents but also other citizens in the community who may have little direct contact with the schools. Often the reasons given for involving community citizens is that they are taxpayers and therefore have a financial stake in the schools' success and because the schools are training the future workers for the community's businesses and industries. But these are superficial reasons. A community's citizens have a stake in the success of the schools because, fundamentally, the schools are teaching the young people of the community how to become viable citizens.

This societal education, in turn, is one reason why educators should strive to resolve diversity issues in the school. Diversity issues that arise in the microcosm of the school mirror such issues in the macrocosm of the community. A societal education that does not include addressing diversity issues and solving problems rooted in diversity conflicts in the school will be incomplete. What happens outside the school is another matter. In this regard, teachers must be viewed as reformers and respected for their insights into the instructional processes that will facilitate such problem solving. Forming partnerships with parents and other community citizens may serve not only to assist in solving diversity problems in the school but also to replicate those solutions in the community.

In a free, democratic society, individuals have the right to pursue their interests. The pursuit of self-interests, however, must be tempered by civility and respect for the rights of others to engage in similar pursuits. The U.S. Constitution and Bill of Rights, the Canadian Charter of Rights and Freedoms, and similar guiding documents in other democratic nations set down principles speaking to the need for balance between the rights of individuals and the rights of collectivities, such as the community or the nation. Such balance is constantly being negotiated. Civility is necessary for successful negotiation. Schools must be active participants in this societal dialogue, and educators must teach their students how to participate in the dialogue.

Universal education is thus an education for civil engagement that likewise balances the goal of helping students learn how to think and do for themselves. One of our goals as educators is to teach students to understand and respect others who may be different from them in terms of culture, race, religious beliefs, gender, sexual orientation, and so on. Learning autonomy, intellectual effectiveness, cultural efficacy, and a disposition for lifelong learning are important touchstones for universal education aimed at developing viable individuals.

Finally, schools must attend to both the micro- and macrocosmic impulses of community. They must be viable communities in themselves, but they also must be exemplars assisting students to become responsible citizens in a free society. To do so, educators must address diversity issues that often stand in the way of achieving community and must solve problems that arise from diversity-based disputes. Teaching for diversity requires not only that teachers understand and deal effectively with the differences before them in the classroom, but also that they teach their students to understand and respect the diversity of individuals in the world around them, whether they are in school or out. (See chapter 9 for curriculum about others.)

Conclusion

No one knows exactly what the future holds, but one thing seems certain: diversity is a fact of life in the 21st century. It has always existed, however much it has been ignored, minimized, or subordinated. The emergence of the information age simply has made—or will make—everyone more aware of human differences. I hope it also serves to raise awareness about what we hold in common across cultures.

Educators will be ever more challenged in years to come to help students understand the human variations in the world around them. They cannot confine teaching merely to the diversity represented among the students in their individual classrooms—though some classrooms of students may be very diverse indeed. In addition, they cannot ignore the global diversity of a world being shrunk by advanced technology, particularly in communication and transportation. Twenty-first century students are not merely citizens of their classroom village or even of their town or nation; they are citizens of the world.

As world citizens, today's classrooms should engage with the issues raised by diversity. Tolerance and acceptance of diversity are stronger when undergirded by awareness and sensitivity. Students need to acquire knowledge about aspects of diversity, such as ethnicity, race, class, sex, gender, sexual orientation, religion, and ability. Such knowledge will be most effectively acquired not in isolated cultural studies but in context—as students work independently and interdependently studying the subject matter of history, literature, the arts, science, and mathematics, and as they learn how to resolve conflicts. I like what famed physicist Albert Einstein once said:

> Something more is needed to produce a truly educated person—namely, an ever-present feeling of social responsibility for fellow human beings. . . . If [teachers] are able to teach young people to have a critical mind and a socially oriented attitude, they will have done all that is necessary. (1968, p. 310)

"A critical mind and a socially oriented attitude" captures well the substance of this book. Teaching for diversity, as I hope I have demonstrated, consists of related strategies that, taken as a whole, will foster intellectual development and help engender a capacity for critical and creative thinking regarding issues of cultural diversity, appearances, language, and situations; for weighing information against values and beliefs, observations and stereotypes; for synthesizing knowledge and creating meaning; and for evaluating diversity without prejudice. These skills are critical for success today and in the century ahead; they are important in school and in the outside world.

Reflections

This chapter serves to synthesize the book's themes as a way to build a learning community in the classroom. Thus, these reflection questions provide readers reflection opportunities to apply and synthesize some of those themes:

1. An effective learning community is clear about its common purpose. Review chapters 1 and 2 about the common purposes of education in a free society. Then discuss how the broader ideas apply to the common purpose of the classroom. Remember that purposes are ideals one strives to make realities.

2. An effective learning community provides its members stability. In the context of a classroom, stability translates to rules and regulations that serve to guide everybody's behavior. Throughout the text, the notion of e pluribus unum has been described as the nation's motto, and in another sense, how it provides the United States a way of recognizing individual rights within a diverse society. Consider how e pluribus unum might provide a philosophic basis for a classroom community. Then extrapolate the philosophy into actual rules and regulations for an effective classroom community.

3. A classroom learning community functions within the context of a school. Reflect on some of the challenges teachers confront in their schools due to physical and social factors. For example, some schools are large with a large student body. Others are tiny but may have attached or unattached outbuildings. Both types of physical layouts could isolate classrooms by either size or location. Social factors may also pose challenges, often related to a school's location within a city or town. Or, the school may

be located far from a city or village. Identify a school and get permission from its principal to study the school for purposes of learning how that school organizes itself so that individual classroom communities are not isolated from the greater school community. If you are in a school, then study how the school links individual classrooms to the greater school community. Before you start the study, think about what you are asking and remember you are a guest in a unique, special community. Be tactful. You are not looking for faults or problems. Rather, you are trying to understand how a school works interdependently.

Stand and Deliver

We live in dynamic times. Teachers must be intellectually dynamic, and they must help students realize a similar dynamism. You are challenged to stand and deliver, an exercise in critical thinking. Reflect on, discuss, weigh, and consider the event. Then, using the key concepts of the chapter, address the questions posed after the scenario.

Bologna and Ketchup

Niki Buska, a sixth grader, has been transferred from her lower-class neighborhood school to an upper-middle-class neighborhood school as part of the school district's desegregation effort. Niki's father works in an iron foundry, and Niki has little in common with her classmates, most of whose fathers work in offices.

Behind her back, the students laugh at her Wal-Mart clothing and street-tough language. She is not obscene, just very direct—and Niki often speaks up without raising her hand to get the teacher's permission. Besides her abrupt speaking style, she does not otherwise bother anyone. At recess, she plays alone on the swings and other playground equipment because none of the other students in her class will play with her.

One day as the students were preparing to go to lunch, Dick raised his hand and spoke over the noisy bustle of the class: "Mrs. Brooks, someone stole my lunch!"

A sudden hush fell over the class as attention turned to Mrs. Brooks and Dick.

Startled to hear the news, she asked, "Where was it?"

"Right here, under my desk in a brown bag," Dick said, looking through the disorganized books and tablets under his desk.

Mrs. Brooks rubbed her brow, puzzled about the missing lunch bag and asked, "What did you have in it?"

Proudly, Dick proclaimed, "I had two bologna sandwiches—with ketchup."

"Yu-u-ck!" Niki blurted. Everybody laughed as she gasped, holding her stomach as though she were ill. "Bologna with ketchup. Yuck!"

Dick shrugged. He said, "I like ketchup. There was a bag of cookies in it, too."

Again, the class fell silent, everyone gazing at Mrs. Brooks. After what seemed a long while, another student, Jane, piped up, saying, "Mrs. Brooks, I saw Niki take his bag."

Niki protested, shaking her head. She said, "No way! I don't like bologna with ketchup!"

Again, a burst of laughter, only now the laughter was nervous, anticipating something dire coming from Mrs. Brooks. But nothing happened. She was overwhelmed by the entire affair. This had never happened in her class, and suddenly she was in the position of judge and jury. The awkward pause continued, but it felt more like being a referee in a basketball game.

Another student, Sally, gingerly said, "I saw Niki stick the bag under her desk."

Mrs. Brooks sharply glanced at Niki, and said, "Niki, let me have your lunch bag."

Not to be threatened, Niki defended herself. "Hey, buzz off! I got rights!"

Mrs. Brooks insisted, "Now, Niki, give me the bag!"

Niki refused. Mrs. Brooks dashed at Niki and grabbed Niki's bag. A tug-of-war erupted, with Mrs. Brooks pulling the top of the bag and Niki pulling away. As Niki tried to jerk it away, the bag ripped, and the food inside splattered into the air and onto the floor. Niki's lunch scattered: two burritos and an apple. Also on the floor were two bologna sandwiches and a bag of cookies.

Niki was upset, whining, "Hey, you spilled my lunch all over the floor!"

Mrs. Brooks was peeved. "Well! The nerve!" Mrs. Brooks coldly exclaimed. "There's Dick's lunch, too!"

Niki was crestfallen, stumped at seeing the bologna sandwich on the floor. She sputtered, "I don't know how it got in my bag, Mrs. Brooks. Honest, I ain't lying."

Mrs. Brooks glared at Niki. Then in a controlled, stern tone, she reprimanded Niki, saying, "I don't know what to do with you, Niki. We've tried hard to get along with you. Now you steal Dick's lunch."

"I didn't take it!" Niki protested. "I don't even like bologna and ketchup!"

Mrs. Brooks was adamant. "Well, the rest of us are going to lunch now," she said. "Dick, I'll get you a hot lunch in the cafeteria. Niki, by the time we get back, I want this mess cleaned up. You'll have time to think about telling the truth."

The other students and Mrs. Brooks proceeded to the cafeteria, while Niki stayed behind in the classroom.

Author's Comments

Mrs. Brooks reflected on the incident and realized she had missed a teachable moment. Everything happened so fast, and she had no idea why she so quickly rushed to judgment. She allowed the heat of the moment to cloud her otherwise calm demeanor. What really happened? Did Niki steal the lunch? Or did someone else put it in her bag? How should she have handled the situation, given that Niki was the newest member of the classroom community? Is it possible somebody else was testing the new kid? In the past when issues arose (this was the most onerous to date), she relied on her intuition without giving much thought to the consequences of her decisions. Now she felt badly. She had missed an opportunity and perhaps acted unjustly. She reflected: "I was the adult in the situation, but my behavior was not befitting the leader of the classroom community." Determined to never let that happen again, she decided it was time to consciously form a learning community in her classroom.

Your Challenge

You do the same. Using the key ideas of this chapter, develop a plan for establishing and maintaining a learning community in the classroom. Be thorough about forming a common purpose, maintaining stability, fostering cooperation, and balancing independence and interdependence. Be specific how you would achieve the common elements of the village. What is your plan to ensure community in the classroom?

References and Resources

Addams, J. (1907). *Democracy and social ethics.* New York: Macmillan.

Adler, M. J. (1982). *The paideia proposal: An educational manifesto.* New York: Macmillan.

Adler, M. J., & Wolff, P. (1959). *General introduction to the great books and to a liberal education.* Chicago: Encyclopedia Britannica.

Archibald, S. (2006). Narrowing in on educational resources that do affect student achievement. *Peabody Journal of Education, 81*(4), 23–42.

Ashton-Warner, S. (1963). *Teacher.* New York: Simon & Schuster.

Au, K. H. (1993). *Literacy instruction in multicultural settings.* Fort Worth, TX: Harcourt Brace.

Baker, J. (2002). *How homophobia hurts children: Nurturing diversity at home, at school, and in the community.* New York: Harrington Park Press.

Balkcom, S. (1992). *Cooperative learning: Education research consumer guide.* Washington, DC: Government Printing Office.

Banks, C. A. (2005). *Improving multicultural education: Lessons from the intergroup education movement.* New York: Teachers College Press.

Banks, J. (Ed.). (1972). The imperatives of ethnic education. *Phi Delta Kappan, 53*(5), 263–268.

Banks, J. (1973). *Teaching ethnic studies: Concepts and strategies.* Washington, DC: National Council for the Social Studies.

Barrett, D., Kurian, G. T., & Johnson, T. M. (2001). *World Christian encyclopedia: A comparative survey of churches and religions in the modern world.* New York: Oxford University Press.

Beck, I., McKeown, M., & Kucan, L. (2002). *Bringing words to life: Robust vocabulary instruction.* New York: Guilford Press.

Brenner, B. (1978). *Wagon wheels.* New York: Harper & Row.

Bruchac, J. (1991). *Native American stories.* Golden, CO: Fulcrum Press.

Cabeza de Baca, F. (1954). *We fed them cactus.* Albuquerque: University of New Mexico Press.

Canadian Multiculturalism Act, c. 31 R. S. C. (4th Supp.) (1985).

Chartock, R. K. (2010). *Strategies and lessons for culturally responsive teaching: A primer for K-12 teachers.* Boston: Pearson.

Clark, K. (1955). *Prejudice and your child.* Boston: Beacon Press.

Clark, K. (1989). *Dark ghetto: Dilemmas of social power.* Middletown, CT: Wesleyan University Press.

Collins, K. (2006, August 4). Salsa grows as condiment and healthy side dish. Accessed at www.msnbc.msn.com/id/14126756/ns/health-diet_and_nutrition on February 18, 2011.

Cothron, J., Giese, R., & Rezba, R. (1996). *Science experiments by the hundreds.* Dubuque, IA: Kendall/Hunt.

Cortés, C. E. (2000). *The children are watching: How the media teach about diversity.* New York: Teachers College Press.

Demo, D., Allen, K., & Fine, M. (2000). *Handbook of family diversity.* New York: Oxford University Press.

Dewey, J. (1902). *The child and the curriculum.* Chicago: University of Chicago Press.

Dewey, J. (1933). *How we think: A restatement of the relation of reflective thinking to the educative process.* Boston: D.C. Heath.

Dewey, J. (1938). *Experience and education.* New York: Macmillan.

Downs, R. (1974). *Horace Mann: Champion of public schools.* New York: Twayne.

Du Bois, W. E. B. (1903). *The soul of black folks: Essays and sketches.* Chicago: A. C. McClurg.

Dudley, J. I. E. (1992). *Choteau Creek: A Sioux reminiscence.* Lincoln: University of Nebraska Press.

DuFour, R., Eaker, R., & DuFour, R. (Eds.). (2008). *On common ground: The power of professional learning communities.* Bloomington, IN: Solution Tree Press.

Echevarria, J., Vogt, M., & Short, D. (2004). *Making content comprehensible for English learners: The SIOP model* (2nd ed.). Boston: Allyn & Bacon.

Einstein, A. (1968). *On education: A speech to the New Jersey Education Association.* In O. Nathan & H. Norden (Eds.), *Einstein on peace* (pp. 308–314). New York: Schocken Books.

Erdoes, R., & Ortiz, A. (Eds.). (1984). *American Indian myths and legends.* New York: Pantheon Books.

Erkens, C., Jakicic, C., Jessie, L. G., King, D., Kramer, S. V., Many, T. W., et al. (2008). *The collaborative teacher: Working together as a professional learning community.* Bloomington, IN: Solution Tree Press.

Families and Advocates Partnership for Education. (2004). *IDEA 2004 summary.* Accessed at www.fape.org/idea/2004/summary.htm on February 24, 2011.

Fermanich, M., & Kimball, S. (2002). You CAN get there from here: How three urban schools could use existing resources to afford comprehensive school reform. *Journal of Education Finance, 28*(1), 75–96.

Franklin, B. (2004). To Peter Collinson (May 9, 1753). In A. Houston (Ed.), *Franklin: The autobiography and other writings on politics, economics, and virtue* (pp. 228–233). Cambridge, UK: Cambridge University Press.

Freire, P. (1970). *Pedagogy of the oppressed.* New York: Herder and Herder.

Froebel, F. (1977). *Education of man.* Washington, DC: University Publications of America.

Gándara, P., & Contreras, F. (2009). *The Latino education crisis: The consequences of failed social policies.* Cambridge, MA: Harvard University Press.

García, R. L. (2011). *Where do cowboys come from? The Mexican roots of the American cowboy.* Lincoln, NE: Nebraska Humanities Council.

Gardner, H., & Hatch, T. (1989). Educational implications of the theory of multiple intelligences. *Educational Researcher, 18*(8), 4–10.

Gay, G. (2000). *Culturally responsive teaching: Theory, research, and practice.* New York: Teachers College Press.

Gay, Lesbian and Straight Education Network. (2010). *The 2009 National School Climate Survey.* Accessed at www.glsen.org on February 23, 2011.

Gibson, P. (1989). Gay male and lesbian youth suicide. In *Report of the secretary's task force on youth suicide* (Vol. 3). Washington, DC: U.S. Government Printing Office.

Gies, F., & Gies, J. (1990). *Life in a medieval village.* New York: Harper & Row.

Good, C. V. (Ed.). (1945). *Dictionary of education, prepared under the auspices of Phi Delta Kappa.* New York: McGraw-Hill.

Goodlad, J. (1984). *A place called school.* New York: McGraw-Hill.

Gordon, M. (1964). *Assimilation in American life: The role of race, religion, and national origins.* New York: Oxford University Press.

Gorski, P. C. (2005). *Multicultural education and the Internet: Intersections and integrations.* Boston: McGraw-Hill.

Gould, S. J. (1981). *The mismeasure of man.* New York: W. W. Norton.

Grady, K. (2002). Lowrider art and Latino students in the rural Midwest. In S. Wortham, E. Murillo, Jr., & E. Hamann (Eds.), *Education in the new Latino diaspora: Policy and the politics of identity* (pp. 169–191). Westport, CT: Ablex.

Grant, M. (1970). *The passing of the great race*. New York: Arno Press.

Harris, N. (1992). A philosophical basis for an Afrocentric orientation. *Western Journal of Black Studies, 16*(3), 154–159.

Harvard Business School Library. (2009). *Hawthorne effect*. Accessed at www.library .hbs.edu/hc/hawthorne on April 20, 2011.

Higham, J. (1963). *Strangers in the land: Patterns of American nativism*. New York: Atheneum.

Hing, B. O. (2004). *Defining America through immigration policy*. Philadelphia: Temple University Press.

Hirsch, E. D. (1987). *Cultural literacy: What every American needs to know*. Boston: Houghton Mifflin.

Johnson, D. (1973). Crime patterns in Philadelphia, 1840–1970. In A. F. Davis and M. Haller (Eds.), *The peoples of Philadelphia: A history of ethnic groups and lower-class life, 1790–1940* (pp. 89–110). Philadelphia: Temple University Press.

Johnson, D. W., & Johnson, R. T. (2010). Cooperative learning and conflict resolution. In J. Bellanca & R. Brandt (Eds.), *21st century skills: Rethinking how students learn* (pp. 201–219). Bloomington, IN: Solution Tree Press.

Johnson, D. W., Johnson, R. T., & Holubec, E. J. (1988). *Cooperation in the classroom*. Edina, MN: Interaction Books.

Kay, K. (2010). Foreword. In J. Bellenca & R. Brandt (Eds.), *21st century skills: Rethinking how students learn* (p. xviii). Bloomington, IN: Solution Tree Press.

Kinsey, A. (1953). *Sexual behavior and the human female*. Philadelphia: Saunders.

Knobel, D. T. (1996). *America for the Americans: The nativist movement in the United States*. New York: Twayne.

Koppelman, K. L., & Goodhart, R. L. (2005). *Understanding human differences: Multicultural education for a diverse America*. Boston: Allyn & Bacon.

Larkin, J. M., & Sleeter, C. E. (1995). *Developing multicultural teacher education curricula*. Rowley, MA: Newbury House.

Lau v. Nichols, 414 U.S. 563 (1974).

Legal Information Institute. (n.d.). *United States Constitution*. Accessed at http:// topics.law.cornell.edu/constitution/billofrights on February 18, 2011.

Lindner, E. W. (Ed.). (2009). *Yearbook of American and Canadian churches*. Nashville, TN: Abingdon Press.

Maccoby, E. E., & Jacklin, C. (1974). *The psychology of sex difference.* Palo Alto, CA: Stanford University Press.

Madsen, J., & Mabokela, R. (2005). *Culturally relevant schools: Creating positive workplace relationships and preventing intergroup differences.* New York: RoutledgeFalmer.

Manning, L. M., & Baruth, L. G. (2009). *Multicultural education of children and adolescents.* Boston: Pearson.

McEwan-Adkins, E. K. (2010). *40 reading intervention strategies for K–6 students: Research-based support for RTI.* Bloomington, IN: Solution Tree Press.

McKee, R., & Davis, J. (2010). *Interpreting in multilingual, multicultural contexts.* Washington, DC: Gallaudet University Press.

McLuhan, M., & Powers, B. R. (1989). *The global village: Transformations in world life and media in the 21st century.* New York: Oxford University Press.

Mélendez, W., & Beck, V. (2010). *Teaching young children in multicultural classrooms.* Belmont, CA: Wadsworth.

Montessori, M. (1917). *The advanced Montessori method.* New York: Frederick A. Stokes.

Montessori, M. (1972). *Education and peace.* Chicago: Henry Regnery.

Muhammad, A. (2009). *Transforming school culture: How to overcome staff division.* Bloomington, IN: Solution Tree Press.

Murillo, E. G., Jr. (2002). How does it feel to be a problem? "Disciplining" the transnational subject in the American South. In S. Wortham, E. G. Murrillo, Jr., & E. T. Hamann (Eds.), *Education in the new Latino diaspora: Policy and the politics of identity* (pp. 215–240). Westport, CT: Ablex.

Murillo, N. (1996). George I. Sanchez and Mexican American educational practices. In J. A. Banks (Ed.), *Multicultural education, transformative knowledge, and action: Historical and contemporary perspectives* (pp. 129–145). New York: Teachers College Press.

Nabozny v. Podlesney, 92 F. 3d 446 (7th Cir. 1996).

Nation, I. S. P. (2001). *Learning vocabulary in another language.* Cambridge, UK: Cambridge University Press.

National Center for Education Statistics. (2004). *Trends in educational equity of girls and women, 2004.* Accessed at http://nces.ed.gov/pubs2005/equity/Section4.asp on February 22, 2011.

National Center for Education Statistics. (2009). *The condition of education.* Washington, DC: U.S. Department of Education.

National Clearinghouse for English Language Acquisition. (n.d.). *National Clearinghouse for English Language Acquisition.* Accessed at www.ncela.gwu.edu on October 12, 2009.

Orozco-Suárez, C., Orozco-Suárez, M., & Todorova, I. (2008). *Learning a new land: Immigrant students in American society.* Cambridge, MA: Harvard University Press.

Padover, S. K. (Ed.). (1939). *Thomas Jefferson on democracy.* New York: Pelican Press.

Pareja, F. (1992). Confessional in the Castilian and Timuquana languages. In D. Weber (Ed.), *The Spanish frontier in North America* (pp. 108–110). New Haven, CT: Yale University Press.

Passel, J. S., & Cohn, D. (2011). *Unauthorized immigrant population: National and state trends, 2010.* Washington, DC: Pew Hispanic Center. Accessed at http://pewhispanic.org/files/reports/133.pdf on March 14, 2011.

Peregoy, S. F., & Boyle, O. F. (2001). *Reading, writing & learning in ESL: A resource book for K–12 teachers* (3rd ed.). New York: Longman.

Pérez, A. I. (2000). *My very own room.* San Francisco: Children's Book Press.

Pew Hispanic Center. (2009). *Immigration.* Accessed at http://pewhispanic.org/topics/?TopicID=16 on February 16, 2011.

Pickering, D. (2010). Teaching the thinking skills that higher-order tasks demand. In R. J. Marzano (Ed.), *On excellence in teaching* (pp. 145–166). Bloomington, IN: Solution Tress Press.

Qoyawayma, P. (1964). *No turning back: A true account of a Hopi Indian girl's struggle to bridge the gap between the world of her people and the world of the white man.* Albuquerque: University of New Mexico Press.

Robles de Meléndez, W. J., & Beck, V. (2010). *Teaching young children in multicultural classrooms: Issues, concepts, and strategies* (3rd ed.). Belmont, CA: Cengage Learning.

Rodrigues, R. J. (2007). *Memoir of a green mountain boy.* New York: iUniverse.

Rousseau, J.-J. (1979). *Emile: On education.* New York: Basic Books.

Sanchez, G. I. (1940). *The forgotten people: A study of New Mexicans.* Albuquerque: University of New Mexico Press.

Sapon-Shevin, M. (2010). *Because we can change the world: A practical guide to building cooperative, inclusive classroom communities.* Thousand Oaks, CA: Corwin Press.

Scieszka, J., & Smith, L. (1989). *The true story of the 3 little pigs!* New York: Viking Kestrel.

Sharan, S., Kussell, P., Hertz-Lazarowitz, R., Bejarano, Y., Raviv, S., & Sharan, Y. (1984). *Cooperative learning in the classroom: Research in desegregated schools.* Mahwah, NJ: Erlbaum.

Sheets, R. H. (2005). *Diversity pedagogy: Examining the role of culture in the teaching-learning process.* Boston: Pearson.

Slavin, R. (1983). *Cooperative learning.* New York: Longman.

Teachers of English to Speakers of Other Languages. (1997). *ESL standards for pre-K–12 students.* Bloomington, IL: Pantagraph.

Thelen, H. A. (1954). *Dynamics of groups at work.* Chicago: University of Chicago Press.

Tileston, D. W., & Darling, S. K. (2008). *Why culture counts: Teaching children of poverty.* Bloomington, IN: Solution Tree Press.

Title IX, Education Amendments of 1972, 20 U.S.C. §1681–1688 (1972).

Tracey, D. H., & Morrow, L. M. (2006). *Lenses on reading: An introduction to theories and models.* New York: Guilford Press.

Truman, H. S. (1965). *Memoirs of Harry S. Truman, 1946–1952.* New York: Da Capo Press.

University of Nebraska State Museum, & Nebraska 4-H Youth Development. (2001). African plant explorer. In University of Nebraska State Museum & Nebraska 4-H Youth Development (Series Eds.), *Wonderwise: Women in science learning series.* Accessed at http://wonderwise.unl.edu/14africa/afrsite.htm on March 11, 2011.

Urban Institute. (2002). *Legal status of the foreign-born population.* Accessed at www.urban.org/publications/p.2 on March 11, 2011.

U.S. Census Bureau. (2005, August 11). *U.S. Census Bureau news.* Washington, DC: U.S. Department of Commerce.

U.S. Census Bureau. (2009). *Income, poverty and health insurance in the United States: 2009.* Accessed at www.census.gov/hhes/www/poverty/data/incpovhlth/2009/index.html on December 13, 2010.

Wilson, J. (1987). *The truly disadvantaged: The inner city, the underclass, and public policy.* Chicago: University of Chicago Press.

Zigler, E. (2010). *The hidden history of Head Start.* New York: Oxford University Press.

Index

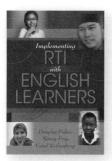

Implementing RTI With English Learners
Douglas Fisher, Nancy Frey, and Carol Rothenberg
Learn why response to intervention (RTI) is the ideal framework for supporting English learners. Follow the application and effectiveness of RTI through the stories of four representative students. **BKF397**

Closing the RTI Gap: Why Poverty and Culture Count
Donna Walker Tileston
Get a clear understanding of poverty and culture, and learn how RTI can close achievement gaps related to these issues. Learn how you can achieve successful implementation in your school. Examine common pitfalls to avoid in the process. **BKF330**

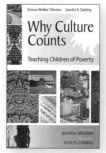

Why Culture Counts: Teaching Children of Poverty
Donna Walker Tileston and Sandra K. Darling
Foreword by Belinda Williams
Afterword by Rosilyn Carroll
Learn how to use students' cultural assets to close the achievement gap with these research-based methods of differentiating the context, content, and process of instruction. **BKF255**

You've Got to Reach Them to Teach Them: Hard Facts About the Soft Skills of Student Engagement
Mary Kim Schreck
Navigate the hot topic of student engagement with a true expert. Become empowered to demand an authentic joy for learning in your classroom. Real-life notes from the field, detailed discussions, practical strategies, and space for reflection complete this essential guide to student engagement. **BKF404**

Solution Tree | Press

a division of
Solution Tree

Visit solution-tree.com or call 800.733.6786 to order.